Foreword

*I*n 1967, I came across a piece of two-thousand-year-old advice from the philosopher Socrates: *Know thyself.* The secret to happiness in life was to know yourself. I spent the next 20 years figuring out what that meant for me and came up with an answer that has been very useful for many other people as well. *Unique Ability.* Based on my own self-improvement and insights from thousands of other individuals, I was able to devise a very simple approach to human learning, growth, success, and satisfaction that seems to work for everyone who is willing to try it. The Unique Ability concept is easy to grasp, makes life immediately more enjoyable, contributes enormously to improved communication and cooperation, produces results in the world that keep getting better, and makes personal happiness a daily reality instead of a wish. Here's the basic idea:

Each of us is born with a potential Unique Ability that has four characteristics: First, it is a superior ability that other people notice and value; second, we love doing it and want to do it as much as possible; third, it is energizing both for us and others around us; and, fourth, we keep getting better, never running out of possibilities for further improvement.

Do some imagining with me. Imagine that from an early age, you had a growing clarity about what you were really great at in life — and that your whole life could be organized around the never-ending development of that ability. As this ability grows, so does your sense of confidence about how you can contribute best to a greater number of people. As a result of this growing contribution, you are constantly rewarded with increasing income, resources, and opportunities. This continually inspires and motivates you to develop your ability even more so that you can make an even greater contribution. Now imagine being surrounded by dozens, hundreds, thousands, and millions of other individuals who are growing and contributing in the same fashion. Imagine the impact on the world in every sector of life. Imagine the creativity, innovation, improvements, and breakthroughs that this would introduce into every situation. Finally, imagine that all of this is entirely possible with the concept of Unique Ability. I know it is, because I am seeing it at work all around me in the lives of thousands of individuals.

Everyone to whom I've described the four Unique Ability characteristics immediately understands what I'm talking about. They've had moments, experiences, whole days and weeks in their lives, where they remember operating in their Unique Ability. Some people call it being in "the zone." Others describe it as "flow." Or "on the beam." For most people, these situations have been infrequent, but for a growing number of people, being in their Unique Ability has become a daily way of life, and the results are remarkable. They live with a sense of direction, confidence, and capability that most people would think of as a dream. They are truly people who know themselves in the way Socrates encouraged us all to do. This book describes how Unique Ability can become a conscious, systematic reality in your life.

Notice that I've said we all have a "potential" Unique Ability. The way the world is organized today, most people spend their lives in a state of *potential* Unique Ability, but do not experience it as a practical reality. They have greatness in them, but it rarely comes out. They could contribute extraordinarily to the world, but they only contribute a little. If they do discover their Unique Ability in the course of life, it is either by accident or luck, invariably because of good parenting and teaching. Those who are able to operate according to their Unique Ability immediately stand out as remarkable human beings. Others think of them as "stars" and wish they could be the same way. But those who are not able to identify their Unique Ability lead generally frustrating, wish-filled lives, which are occupied with anger, resentment, self-doubt, and self-criticism.

The main reason for the failure to identify Unique Ability lies in the way that the vast majority of people are conditioned throughout their lives. They are told in a thousand different ways that the purpose of life is to fit in, rather than to stand out. That they need to be acceptable, rather than exceptional. That they need to get along, rather than to get better. That it's more important to be popular than productive. That it's more important to consume than to create. That security is more important than success. That they should have modest aspirations that can be safely met, rather than extraordinary goals that force them to go beyond their present skills. That the future is "scary and uncertain" rather than something they can and will create out of their own dreams and abilities.

All of these negative and limiting messages, which come from parents, siblings, friends, peers, teachers, clerics, employers, colleagues, politicians, bureaucrats, radio, TV, the Internet, movies, newspapers, magazines, popular music, and literature effectively and permanently discourage most people from ever looking inside themselves for their Unique Ability.

Yet everyone who hears about Unique Ability, and learns how to identify it in himself or herself and then articulate it for others, immediately begins to break through all of these psychological and emotional barriers. An individual can have decades of negative programming and overcome it all after just a few years of focusing on his or her Unique Ability. I've seen men and women who first came across the concept of Unique Ability in their sixties and seventies immediately begin to transform their lives and the world around them. This suggests, then, that it is only a matter of exposing as many people as possible to the idea. Their innate desire for personal freedom, growth, contribution, success, and happiness will do the rest.

My own journey to discover my Unique Ability was greatly accelerated by a great question. It was posed to me by my wife and business partner, Babs Smith, at a point in my life when I had had a failed marriage and two bankruptcies within a very short period. I was definitely looking for answers that would help me to get myself on a sure path to greater happiness and success.

"Why are *you* doing that?" she asked one day in reaction to seeing me, yet again, involve myself in some activity without success. "You haven't been successful at business because you're doing all this other stuff. Do what you're really good at, and I'll set up a structure that will handle the rest." As usual, Babs' natural intuitive skills led me straight to the heart of the matter: I was allowing myself to be distracted by all kinds of activities I had no right to be doing. I was terrible at them. They were draining my energy and my confidence. I had little time or "juice" left to work at the things I was really good at. True to her word, Babs began to put together the structure I needed in order to focus all my energies on what I love to do and do best.

I've now been aware of my Unique Ability for 20 years and have continually worked on strengthening its power by surrounding myself with others who are great at doing all the things that lie outside of it. But when I look back over my life, right back to my childhood, I can see my Unique Ability reflected in things I did as young as the age of six.

I grew up on a working farm in Ohio, the middle child with siblings either a number of years older or younger than me. Most of the time, I was among adults or I had to find my own entertainment. One of my "chores" on the farm actually became one of my favorite forms of entertainment — walking to the neighboring farm to pick up milk for my family from Mrs. Wetzel. It was about a five-minute walk, but my visits never lasted less than an hour. I loved to ask Mrs. Wetzel, who was about 75 years old at the time, question after question about her life. She kindly and patiently answered them all. Both of us enjoyed these visits, and Mrs. Wetzel often phoned my mother to say, "Danny was over. We talked, and I feel so much better."

I learned then that life was about asking the right questions and letting people talk about themselves. The bonus was that when I asked the right questions, almost anything was interesting. Asking questions opened up whole new worlds for me. I didn't see myself living my entire life on the farm. I had much bigger plans. Asking the right questions was the key, and is the foundation of my Unique Ability to this day.

In fact, it was through asking questions that I first started to think about and formulate the idea of Unique Ability. The Canadian government declared 1980 the Year of the Disabled. I was hired by a friend, who had recently been elected to Parliament, to interview disabled people across the country and write a report on my findings. Again I was in the role of questioner, and I loved it. I came away from this process with a great revelation. What I discovered during my cross-Canada interviews was that the happiest and most successful of the disabled people I talked with were those who had acknowledged their disability, let others do what they themselves couldn't manage, and focused solely on areas where they could make the greatest contribution. This, really, is the essence of Unique Ability and was the birth of the concept in my mind. All of us are "disabled" in certain areas. Letting go of these areas to focus on the things we love to do and that give us our greatest results is the secret to greater confidence, happiness, success, freedom, and fulfillment.

Looking back, I see that my visits with Mrs. Wetzel and the questions I asked as a six-year-old child were the first step in the development of my career as a coach. I've always maintained that The Strategic Coach Program is really an endless series of questions linked together as concepts, tools, and structures that liberate people to acknowledge, talk about, and deal with things that may be impeding their progress. Mrs. Wetzel was my first "coaching client," but I can see many other instances in my life where my fledgling Unique Ability was at work.

The concept of Unique Ability has become the foundation for how I conduct my life and my work. It is a seminal concept in The Strategic Coach Program, where we help entrepreneurs to discover and then work increasingly in their Unique Ability to achieve their most important lifetime goals. The Strategic Coach company that Babs and I have created is an organization that supports the discovery and growth of each team member's Unique Ability. This book represents Unique Ability at work. It has been developed by a team of uniquely talented individuals at The Strategic Coach: Catherine Nomura, Julia Waller, Shannon Waller, Hamish MacDonald, and Myrna Nemirsky. Each one brought to the project his or her unique passion, skill set, and world experience. When the team was nearing the end of the project, they asked me if I would write the Foreword. It has given me enormous pleasure to do so.

Unique Ability has already proven itself a thousand times over as a tool for personal self-improvement. But I believe it goes far beyond that. Unique Ability goes to the very heart of what human progress has been about for more than 2,000 years, since the time of Socrates. The last 100 years have seen a terrible rebellion on our planet against the very idea of individual freedom that is the driving concept of western civilization. For most of the 20th Century, three terrible ideologies — Fascism, Communism, and Nazism — imprisoned great numbers of people within totalitarian systems opposed to individual liberty.

The Fascist writer Alfredo Rocco, advisor to Mussolini, made the totalitarian agenda utterly clear:

> *For Liberalism (i.e. individualism), the individual is the end and society the means; nor is it conceivable that the individual, considered in the dignity of an ultimate finality, be lowered to mere instrumentality. For Fascism, society is the end, individuals the means, and its whole life consists in using individuals as instruments for its social ends.*
>
> **Alfredo Rocco, advisor to Mussolini**

I firmly believe that a global educational approach based on Unique Ability — on the constant lifetime development of individual uniqueness — will prevent this kind of totalitarian thinking from ever again gaining even a small foothold in human affairs.

Dan Sullivan
November 14, 2003

Introduction

Unique Ability

Creating The Life You Want

Introduction

*U*nique Ability® is a way of describing a powerful force that is at the very core of who you are as an individual. It's a basic part of being human. Every person who has ever lived has had a Unique Ability, though most people haven't been conscious of it. Because of this lack of awareness, most people haven't experienced the infinite rewards that come from being able to harness and develop their natural talents and pursue their passions wholeheartedly. The more you're able to recognize and develop your Unique Ability and shape your life around it, the more freedom, happiness, and success you'll experience — and the better off the rest of the world will be. Talent fueled by passion, especially when it's directed by self-knowledge and focused on creating value, is your greatest personal resource. It's also your best way to make a unique, profound, and lasting positive impact on the world.

What you are about to read will help you understand Unique Ability and focus on yours so you can work on making it stronger and using it in more productive, strategic, and rewarding ways. The concept of Unique Ability is the brainchild of Dan Sullivan and his wife and business partner, Babs Smith. They have spent the last 20 years coaching very successful entrepreneurs on how to break through to new levels of achievement, happiness, and freedom in their personal and professional lives. Their company, The Strategic Coach®, has helped entrepreneurs, their teams, and families experience greater success and freedom largely by finding different ways to support them in discovering and focusing more on their Unique Abilities. This book represents what The

Strategic Coach has learned about Unique Ability, its benefits, and how to discover and harness its power. With all the incredible results we've been fortunate enough to see and experience, we felt it was time to more widely share this understanding and make it accessible to everyone.

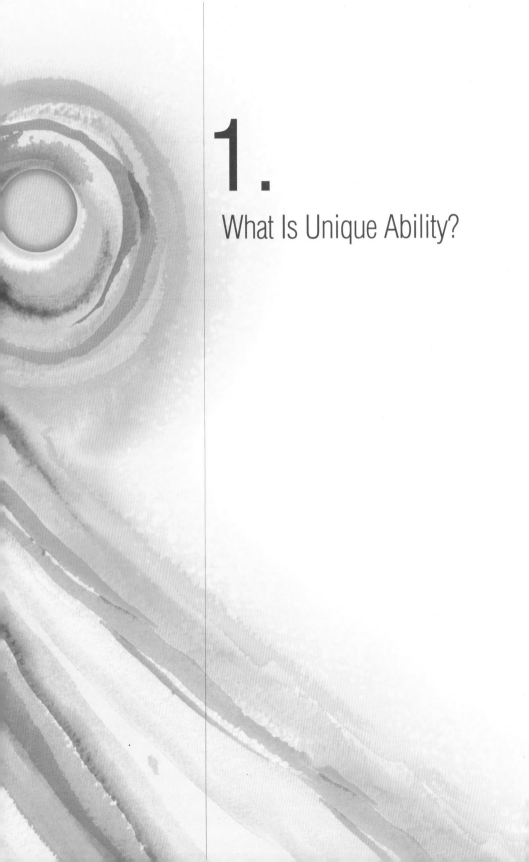

1.

What Is Unique Ability?

Unique Ability

Creating The Life You Want

Chapter 1:
What Is Unique Ability?

A lanky young man decides he can't swing a pick in California's sun-baked clay much longer. It's killing him. At 18, this is not the life he wants for himself, his expectant wife, or their new baby due in a few months. He's here after dropping out of Kalamazoo College in Michigan because he hated it. He is John Hittler. To get people over their discomfort at hearing his name, he says, "I know you're wondering about my name. Let me spell it for you: It's J-O-H-N."

John wants to go to Georgetown University, and study in the acclaimed School of Foreign Service. A degree from Georgetown would certainly open doors to the life he wants. The only problem is that it's August, the school year is about to begin, and he has not even applied, let alone been accepted. Without telling his wife these finer details, they pack up their VW bug and head across the country. John is going to Georgetown.

This is also what he tells the people who greet him in the registration office. "I'm ready to go to the School of Foreign Service," he says.
When they don't find his name on the list, he has to admit that he didn't apply. This prompts them to explain the whole admissions policy to him. No application, no acceptance, no admission.

So he asks, "How many people in the freshman class?"
"Nineteen hundred," they reply. "But only one in 80 even gets accepted to the SFS."

"Well, surely some of them won't show up?"

"Perhaps, but all of the SFS students have matriculated already. There are seven who have been accepted and paid their fees but are not expected to arrive."

"Well which school (there are five colleges at Georgetown) has openings?" John asks."

"The School of Languages and Linguistics has the most openings. They are fully staffed with tenured professors but not fully enrolled, especially the German Department."

"Why don't I just take one of the open spots in the Language School, and major in German?" asks John.

"That's not how it works," and they go through the policy with him again.

After some discussion, he is able to shift the focus to the fact that, without those people, there will be spaces in some classes, so theoretically, he might be able to replace one of them to everyone's benefit.

"But even if you did," they ask, "what are you going to do about housing?"

"Well, aren't all freshmen required to live on campus?" asks John.

"Yes, but they've all been assigned rooms and roommates. You don't even have a roommate."

"Are these roommates people they know already?"

"No, they don't know each other beforehand."

"Well then, I can just walk in and shake someone's hand and introduce myself and we'll be roommates." The other student would have a roommate, and John would have a place to live. The plan was for John to study in Washington, D. C. while his new wife would go on to New York City to study for one semester before their first child is born in the spring. At that point, they would find housing in D.C. and live as a family.

"Well, yes, I guess you could do that."

Together they work through all the systems and procedures for his admission over a period of three days. As various obstacles arise, John comes up with a solution for each one that actually makes it easier for the school or better for the other students, even though it's highly irregular. For instance, when it comes time to figure out how he'll pay his tuition, he asks if any of the students who didn't show up had grants or scholarships. They discover that there are four government grants that are not being claimed. He convinces them to transfer these financial aid funds and all the non-refundable fees paid by people who didn't show up into his account. At least this way, the funds will actually go towards someone's education this year, which was the original intent. No one is worse off, and several people will actually benefit. He's in.

Every semester he was at Georgetown, John went back to the financial aid office and went through the process of figuring out who dropped out, who died, who left for any reason, and got their financial aid and non-refundable money transferred into his account. In four years, he spent a total of about $2,500 of his own money on tuition — not bad for a Jesuit University, traditionally one of the most expensive in the country.

The people at the admissions office and the financial aid office were able to do what they felt was a good deed. And John got his degree from Georgetown without ever formally applying or being accepted. In the end, he graduated from the school of Languages and Linguistics, rather than the School of Foreign Service, with a degree in German and a concentration in economics. Initially, he had planned on studying international economics, with German as his language requirement. Essentially, he did the same curriculum — just from the "wrong" school within Georgetown.

John has a special talent, one that allowed him to turn this situation around — he made it into a game where everyone would win. He describes his Unique

Ability as "designing and articulating really big games, in which the participants all win, simply by playing." This is the essence of what he's doing in all areas of his life where he's most successful.

> Unique Ability is the essence of what you love to do, and do best.

When John first discovered his Unique Ability (he always had it, but didn't always know he had it) he estimates that he was using his Unique Ability about five percent of the time. Since discovering and honing his Unique Ability, he now uses it about 40 percent of the time, and the results have been terrific. Two main results have occurred: First, John's income has gone up four times in the past eight years, since beginning to "play" in his Unique Ability more. He works less, earns more, and has more time to design and play games he's passionate about — like his charitable causes. Second, he has avoided areas of difficulty. John realized that all the times he had gotten into "trouble" in business or in life, he was generally working in a situation where his Unique Ability was not needed or wanted. He now tends to avoid these situations up front, by simply asking himself the question: "Is my Unique Ability needed here or not?" When it's not, he avoids the situation completely. In this manner, he makes a large impact where he can, and allows other people to use their Unique Ability where he cannot. Life is much more enjoyable with that guideline.

On meeting John, it's easy to see that he's always playing in some way or another. Not motivated by small opportunities, he has continued over the years to create games in many different arenas where the stakes are high and the potential winnings large. Now in his forties, John has run several diverse entrepreneurial businesses. He uses his Unique Ability to create brilliantly innovative solutions that motivate and benefit clients and customers, suppliers, and his own teams. Using his unique talents to overcome the many obstacles involved, he and his wife have adopted three orphaned children from Russia. By documenting and sharing the process, he hopes to give more prospective parents the know-how to do the same. With his own family currently at seven children, some biological and some adopted, the only way this game can get significantly bigger is if others get involved. He also creates "games" to help volunteer-based organizations achieve their goals more effectively. In all of these areas, he has a superior talent and intense passion that allow him to be successful in complex situations where there's a lot at stake.

What is Unique Ability?

So what exactly is Unique Ability and how can it be so powerful? Here's a brief definition and description to start; then we'll take you through a process to discover and articulate your own.

Unique Ability is the essence of what you love to do, and do best. There are four characteristics of Unique Ability: It's a superior ability that other people notice and value; you are passionate about using it and want to use it as much as possible; it's energizing both for you and others around you; and there's a sense of never-ending improvement — you keep getting better and better and never run out of possibilities for growth.

Unique Ability:
- Superior ability
- Passion
- Energy
- Never-ending improvement

Because your Unique Ability is fueled by tremendous passion, it can be a very powerful force in the world and create enormous value for others. When you combine talent and passion, you have a recipe for never-ending improvement, energy, excitement, and higher and higher levels of achievement.

Are you sure I have a Unique Ability?

At this point, you may be thinking, "I don't have a Unique Ability." To start with, many people don't see themselves as unique, or special. Let's address that right away. By nature, we're all unique. It's a fact of life that there is nobody else in the world just like you. At a very basic level, we're all different. What you choose to do with your uniqueness and your talents is up to you. You may have tried to "fit in" and as a result have downplayed or suppressed your individuality. Everyone's uniqueness is something to be celebrated and cultivated. What gives your Unique Ability its one-of-a-kind character is that it draws on and combines your innate talents, your personal passion, and your life experience, which no one else can duplicate.

It must be used to be seen.

We describe it as an "ability" because Unique Ability enables you to achieve great results when applied to a range of different activities. It must be used to be seen. Unique Ability shows up exclusively in your interactions with the world. Though the idea of Unique Ability may be a theoretical construct, your actual Unique Ability is very real.

Now, if you combine "unique" with "ability," you may be thinking that, sure, I may be unique, but my abilities really aren't that special. That's the trick with Unique Ability. It comes so naturally, is so easy, fun, energizing, and motivating, we don't think it's special. We think to ourselves, "Can't everyone do that?" The truthful answer is, no, they can't. And certainly not like you do. We're taught to believe that things have to be hard work in order to be valuable. What if we really each have a powerful natural talent and way of operating in the world, that if properly cultivated, expressed, and applied to the right situations could achieve the greatest possible results with relative ease? Doesn't that sound like more fun than continually working on things you're not good at? Unique Ability gives you the chance to do what you love, experience your greatest success, and contribute the most to the world around you.

Unique Ability gives you the chance to do what you love, experience your greatest success, and contribute the most to the world around you.

Another factor that makes it difficult to see your own Unique Ability is that it's mixed in with lots of other kinds of activities. Like most of us, you probably spend a lot of time doing things that simply need to get done to make your life work. You're not passionate about these activities, and you may or may not be great at them — they're just a part of living. Without knowing about Unique Ability, you wouldn't think to differentiate what you love from everything else you do.

After accepting that you have a Unique Ability, the next challenge is figuring out what it is, and how to say it. Getting down to the essence of who you are and what you're about can feel like digging for a needle in a very large haystack. It's essentially trying to articulate who you are. We each have innate wisdom. At some core level, we already know who we are and what we're about. You may have thought a lot about it, or not much at all. As with most things in life, if you're willing to delve in and do some thinking, the answer is there. You just have to be willing to trust the process.

What does my Unique Ability look like?

Unique Ability shapes your whole way of being — it's the "you" that makes you who you are. Your Unique Ability shows up in your skills, your talents, your characteristics, your activities, your creativity, and your habits. These are some of the means by which it comes out, yet it's more than any of these: It's also an expression of your values. If you've ever felt the excitement of doing something you excel at and others praise you for, something you'd happily keep doing all day long, you've probably experienced your Unique Ability in action. Because you use it so naturally and willingly, it's constantly evolving and improving as you move through life. When you give it room and focus on it, that evolution speeds up and the value you create for others increases.

When you use your Unique Ability, time flies.

How do I know when I'm using my Unique Ability?

People often don't recognize when they're using their Unique Ability themselves, but others see it quite clearly. To you it's so natural that you use it and don't even know you're using it. But when you've seen someone else display their Unique Ability, particularly if they've developed and focused on it over a number of years — for instance, a sports star, or a friend with a particular gift — it's immediately obvious. To get your mind thinking in the realm of Unique Ability, here are a few clues to look for as you reflect on your daily activities: When you use your Unique Ability, time flies. When you're focused on the activities that allow your Unique Ability to come out, you love them so much that you could do them all the time and not run out of energy. In fact, doing these things gives you more energy because you're passionate about them. These activities tap into your internal motivation and drive. You may feel like you're able to access or channel energy and creativity that come from a bigger source, that ideas and solutions just flow naturally.

Think back to your childhood: Was there anything you did endlessly that parents or others had to tear you away from for mundane things like meal time or sleep? Unique Ability has exactly that quality about it. Some aspect of what you were drawn to back then is likely still part of your Unique Ability today. The essence of your talent has been at play in your life since childhood — Unique

Ability is "factory-installed." After you go through The Unique Ability Discovery Process in the next chapter, you can look back and see where your Unique Ability has been in action throughout your life.

Unique Ability works.

Your Unique Ability doesn't just keep you happily occupied and give you energy — it works. You generate consistent, high quality results by using it, and the more you use it, the better you get. It may show up in your work, in your hobbies, in all kinds of relationships, and in the things you do with your family, your community, or your friends. In all these areas, it creates value that others recognize. The more you understand what your Unique Ability is and how well it works in different situations, the more you can expand your capacity to use it and reap the benefits. You'll have more fun and energy, experience tremendous growth, create meaningful results, and impact others in a positive and creative way. Pretty good for something that comes so easily.

Here's an example of how someone's Unique Ability works in real life: Karen M. is the team leader of our Chicago office. She describes her Unique Ability as "analyzing the big picture and directing and encouraging people to produce an outstanding result." Anyone in the company who comes in contact with Karen experiences first-hand her probing for information and then her gentle arranging of people and resources, followed by tremendous encouragement: "You can do it." If you ask any of Karen's four children, her husband, or the people in her community marriage class, they'll tell you that she operates in the same fashion. She can be counted on to gather information, then direct everyone to achieve successful results for all involved. This ability to orchestrate people and resources, combined with Karen's passionate commitment to quality results, has led her to be an incredible manager, team builder, counselor, spouse, and mother.

*Working in my Unique Ability is always exciting and energizing
for me. I love the anticipation of the results of an endeavor and
the excitement of the team as we reach new levels of growth.*

Karen M.

A different world view.

Unique Ability is a philosophy and a way of looking at human potential, beginning with your own, and extending to every person in the world. It has many
implications for how we view ourselves and others, and provides a unique sense
of purpose and direction to our lives.

We have also found that, as an idea, it has an infectious quality. Once people
understand the concept and begin to see how it operates in their own lives, they
feel compelled to share it with others. It offers a different perspective and
clarity on issues that many people struggle with.

Everyday uniqueness.

One of the most basic tenets of the philosophy of Unique Ability is that having
a Unique Ability is just an ordinary part of being human. Everybody has one.
In this, we're all equal. What makes it, and you, both special and distinctive is
the extent to which you express your Unique Ability, use it to create value, and
combine it with the Unique Abilities of others. We each have the choice to do
this to a greater or lesser extent and to seek out situations that make it easier
or more difficult. By being aware of the Unique Abilities of others, you gain
access to an incredible resource of human capability driven by passion. For

The idea of Unique Ability is liberating because it allows you to be who
you are, and gives you permission to make your greatest possible contribution to the world by doing what you love to do.

many people, a big change in outlook occurs when they begin to accept as a given that everyone has a Unique Ability, and then to appreciate what each person's Unique Ability is. Great benefit comes from making a habit of developing yours and recognizing others who have developed theirs. When you see this as just part of how the world works, it enables you to tap into and work with your own unique talents and those of others, both on conscious and subconscious levels.

The path to freedom and happiness.

The very idea of Unique Ability is liberating because it allows you to be who you are, and gives you permission to make your greatest possible contribution to the world by doing what you love to do. It allows you to create the life you want. It also has the benefit of freeing each of us from the many negative feelings like guilt, inadequacy, and frustration that arise as we try to do or avoid the things we're not unique at. The flipside to the fact that everyone has a Unique Ability, is that everyone also has areas that are not their Unique Ability. Freedom comes from recognizing and letting go of those activities that don't engage your passion, that don't generate energy, superior results, and never-ending improvement. It's often observed of the world today that people don't suffer from the lack of opportunity, they suffer from too much. They don't have too few options, they have too many. With so many demands on our time and so many choices to be made on a daily basis, the concept of Unique Ability provides a much needed focus. Much of the relief that people experience once they begin to understand their Unique Ability and focus on it comes from the deep inner sense that by focusing in this way, they are maximizing their happiness, freedom, and productivity. In the following chapters of this book, we'll show you how to do exactly that.

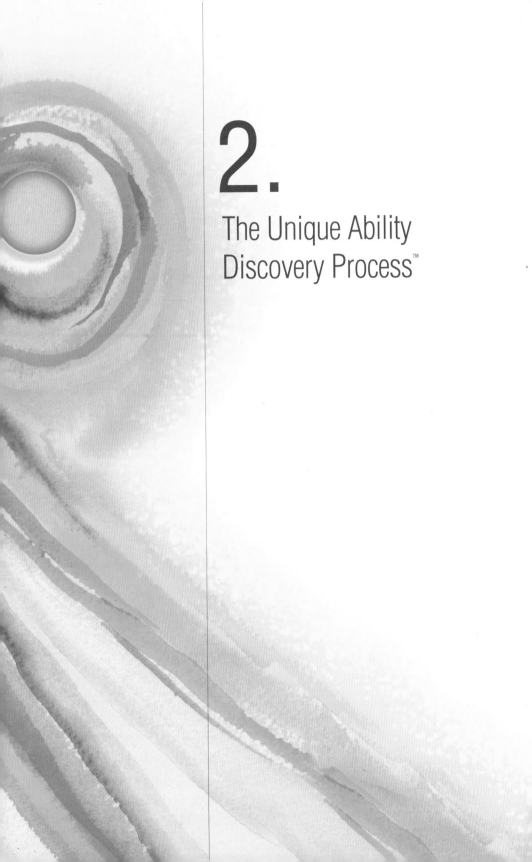

2.

The Unique Ability
Discovery Process™

Unique Ability

Creating The Life You Want

Chapter 2:
The Unique Ability
Discovery Process™

If you deny even one man entrance into your life, you'll never get his uniqueness from anyone else. I, for instance, want you in my life because without you, my life will never be complete. But only when you find the you of you, will you have anything to give me, just as I must find the me of me.

Leo Buscaglia, paraphrasing Buckminster Fuller

A lifelong process of self-discovery.

It's time to discover and define your Unique Ability. A few words here to guide your expectations: This is a lifelong process of revelation and refinement. As soon as you begin, you'll reap some immediate benefits. Your understanding will continue to deepen over time and with experience, bringing greater progress and rewards. As you spend more time using your Unique Ability and being aware of when you're not using it, your articulation of it will evolve to become increasingly precise, refined, and widely applicable. This is normal. You'll talk about your Unique Ability with people who know you well, and their feedback will help you find the words to express it with greater clarity. Every time it evolves, your understanding of your Unique Ability will provide you with more direction and confidence and new insights. Here, at the beginning, you're about to lay the groundwork for all that progress.

You may already have a sense of what your Unique Ability is and be using it consciously on a regular basis. If so, you are one of a lucky few. With the complexities of modern life and the daily activities and relationships we engage in, most people need some assistance to identify and separate where and how their Unique Ability is being used. Being so close to our own uniqueness makes it even more difficult to see. Virtually no one uses his or her Unique Ability all the time. We all need help to use it more. The key is to start by identifying what it is and when and how you are using it, and expand on that.

The next pages will guide you through a proven six-step process that will take you on a journey of self-discovery. The steps are simple, but the process won't necessarily feel easy. Most people aren't used to turning the spotlight on themselves in this way. For instance: Try describing who you are and what you're about in one sentence. Sound like a challenge? Don't worry: The goal is progress, not perfection. This process will get you a first draft — something for you to try out, refine, and build upon from here forward. These steps are the same ones that the people whose comments you see on the inside cover and throughout this book completed. All of these people and many more have worked through this process successfully, overcoming their natural apprehensions and fears along the way, to achieve great results. A critical part of your success will be the people you enlist to help you. Unique Ability may be about you, but it's not something you discover alone.

The Unique Ability Discovery Process.

The following process will clarify your thinking about your Unique Ability and leave you with an action plan to implement right away. The first three exercises are designed to give you a clear sense of how you operate best and what your Unique Ability actually is. Then, in the last three exercises, you'll look at the more practical application of your Unique Ability and where you express it in your work and personal life. Keep in mind that you don't need a perfect result the first time you complete these exercises. There is no "right" answer, only one that works for you now, and one that can be developed and refined as you gain more experience. You may struggle a bit, and that's okay. You'll do a lot

The Unique Ability Discovery Process™

6. **The Unique Ability Action Plan** — Create a plan to maximize the time you spend applying your Unique Ability.

5. **The Activity Snapshot** — Distill and organize your activities by category to become clear about which ones best use your Unique Ability and where you need teamwork and support.

4. **The Activity Inventory** — List, then categorize all the activities in your life to get an overall picture of how you spend your time.

3. **The Unique Ability Statement** — Articulate your Unique Ability — the essence of what you do well and the underlying passion that motivates and drives you — in one simple sentence.

2. **The 10 Best Habits** — Derive a list of your "best habits" — how you consistently get your best results.

1. **The Unique Ability Question** — Ask others in your life for their experience of your Unique Ability.

of thinking that will be useful to you immediately. Then, with more practice, you'll build on your understanding and expression of who you are and take your insights to a deeper level.

The first time you go through the exercises, you'll build a foundation of insight which will open doors to greater self-knowledge and to understanding some of the practical changes you can make to start operating more in your Unique Ability. As time passes, if you feel you'd like to increase your focus even more, the same exercises can be re-used to take you to the next level. You may want to reflect on your initial results to glean new insights, or you may wish to redo some of the exercises. Though the process will be the same, you, your understanding, and your circumstances will be different, so you'll get different results that will reflect your new discoveries and experiences.

To keep all your thoughts in one place, we suggest you get a notebook to use as you complete these exercises. Your Unique Ability Notebook will become a rich storehouse of knowledge, insights, and wisdom that you can refer back to, refine, and add to over time.

A picture of you.

Since your Unique Ability is the essence of who you are, it shows up everywhere in your life. The following exercises will help you gain a perspective on your unique talents, what others value about you, and what always works for you. The process of going through these exercises, then reviewing and knitting together the results, will give you a picture of yourself that is more comprehensive and objective than what any single tool or measure can provide. Think of it as creating a picture on a tapestry woven from many different threads, all of which are uniquely you. This picture will allow you to better see how your unique talents and passion might be applied to a wide range of activities and situations. It is also tremendously self-affirming and confidence-building.

Step 1: The Unique Ability Question™.

Enough about me, what do *you* think about me?

The way to start defining your Unique Ability is to get other people's perspectives on it. The Unique Ability Question is a simple exercise that will help you do this. People who know you well have a certain experience of being with you, and each will have a sense of your special talents. You'll use their observations to let you see from the outside what you have difficulty seeing from the inside.

Going against the grain.

The Unique Ability Question takes the form of a letter or e-mail that you'll send to people you trust, inviting them to give you feedback about your Unique Ability. You might feel uncomfortable at first about asking for input from others about your talents and strengths. Some people think this feels too much like fishing for compliments. Self-deprecation is considered a virtue by many. The school of thought that promotes well-roundedness supports focusing on what you're not so good at, so you may be more conditioned to ask about where you need to improve. However, there's nothing wrong with asking for positive feedback. After all, if we don't know what we're doing that's working, how can we do more of it? The fundamental premise on which the concept of Unique Ability is based is to focus on your strengths and eliminate or delegate your weaknesses as much as possible. If you know what your strengths are, you can reinforce and grow them. Eventually, there won't be much breathing room for your weaknesses — you'll simply cut off their air supply.

It may feel like a risk to ask people what they appreciate and value about you. This is where negative thoughts sometimes come in: "What if they don't value anything about me and they feel like they have to make something up?" or "What if I don't like what they say?" The fact is, you may not get responses from every single person you ask, but the usual reason is that they just didn't have time to pull their thoughts together by your deadline. People tend to take this kind of request seriously, and they want to carefully consider what they say. It's very satisfying to tell someone what you appreciate about them in a safe, appropriate context. Unfortunately, without prompting, we often don't think about saying these things until it's too late — in eulogies and obituaries. Don't be afraid to ask now. This is extremely important raw material for you to use in articulating your Unique Ability. Your Unique Ability is so natural to you that much of it is invisible from your vantage point. Even if you go no further in this process, it's worth doing this one exercise. You'll be touched by people's responses, and they'll enjoy having the opportunity to share their insights with you.

> *The letter was what really got me going with this process. That gave what we were talking about an added level of reality; it wasn't just something I was making up.*
>
> **Hamish M.**

Send the question below in an e-mail or letter to eight to ten people, whose opinions you respect and who know you well. These people can be friends, family members, colleagues, classmates — anyone who has been in a position to see you demonstrate your abilities over time. It's best to paraphrase or change the letter to reflect your own voice so it sounds like you. You may want to be more or less formal or personal, or change the wording — just don't omit the essential question: "What do you see as my Unique Ability?" It's also important to communicate a timeframe in your letter, as undated tasks have a way of slipping down — and off — people's to-do lists.

Here are two examples to refer to when writing your own Unique Ability Question:

Dear Suzanne,

I am currently reading a book about a concept called Unique Ability. This concept is based on the idea that everyone possesses a combination of talents, interests, and capabilities unique to that individual.

I'd really appreciate it if you would help me identify my own Unique Ability by considering the following question and sending me back an answer: "What do you see as my Unique Ability?" My Unique Ability includes my talents and abilities, characteristics that describe me, what I'm good at, how I do things, what you count on me for, and any other distinguishing features you see about who I am.

I'd be very grateful if you could respond within the next two weeks if you're interested in helping me. Thanks for your support. I look forward to hearing from you.

All the best,

Frances

From: ___ Chris

Subject: ___ Unique Ability

To: ___ Joe

Cc: ___

Hi Joe,

I have what might seem like a strange favor to ask you. I'm reading a book about a concept called Unique Ability: It's based on the idea that everyone has a unique set of talents, interests, and capabilities that they're passionate about, and that can be used to create a lot of value in the world.

I'm trying to find out what mine is. So, because I value your opinion, I was wondering if you could think about this question and send me back an answer: "What do you see as my Unique Ability?" My Unique Ability includes my talents and abilities, characteristics that describe me, what I'm good at, how I do things, what you count on me for, and any other distinguishing features you see about who I am.

It would really help me out if you could get back to me in the next two weeks with any thoughts you might have on this. Thanks so much.

Cheers,
Chris

Take it all in.

Once you've received the responses to your Unique Ability Question, read them through and enjoy what people said. You may not be used to reading so many good things about yourself! This first exercise will show you in a very concrete way how your strengths and talents are perceived and appreciated by those around you.

Look for patterns.

After enjoying and absorbing the feedback you've received, read through the responses again and look for patterns in what people said. Examine the ways people chose to describe your Unique Ability. Start a page in your notebook and label it "The Unique Ability Question." List each person's name and identify the key words or phrases they used that really hit home for you. Once you've gone through all the responses, look back and take note of any recurring words, phrases, or ideas. These themes are keys to your Unique Ability and will be invaluable in the next exercises.

> *I'm not the one who stated what my Unique Ability is. It came from colleagues, friends, and family. That was the enlightening part: These people from different realms of my life all said the same thing.*
> **Katherine E.**

> *The feedback that I got was very useful and insightful, and it gave people a chance to really think about and express who they see me to be and what they appreciate about me. The parallels in the responses were startling.*
> **Dave N.**

It's validating to find out what others appreciate about you. You may even discover that the things they most value are not what you expected. This is all great input, but feeling good is not the purpose of the exercise, just a happy by-product. The purpose is to give you a source of raw material to mine for clues to your Unique Ability. Other people's words and insights will help you get clearer on how you create value using your Unique Ability. They're the ones you're creating value for, and value creation is always in the eye of the beholder.

More raw material highly recommended.

At The Strategic Coach, we have also found two tools created by other organizations to be very helpful in illuminating Unique Ability. These are the Kolbe A Index from Kolbe Corp, and the StrengthsFinder profile from The Gallup Organization. These profiles help create a more detailed picture of your Unique Ability. Each requires that you answer a series of questions that take about 20 to 40 minutes to complete. A personal profile based on your answers will provide more insight into how you go about achieving successful results in all areas of your life. Both of these tools measure only strengths — there are no wrong answers or "bad" results.

The Kolbe A* Index.

The Kolbe A Index will give you a greater understanding about how a very important part of your mind works that you may not even know exists. Kathy Kolbe describes three parts of the human mind: the cognitive part, which has to do with knowledge and intellect, often measured by IQ tests; the affective part, which has to do with feelings, emotions, values, and personality; and the less-known conative part, which governs our striving instincts, or how we go about getting things done. The Kolbe Index (*www.kolbe.com*) measures your striving instincts, which are an important factor in your behavior, in the mental energy you have for certain tasks, and in how you approach these tasks. These instincts remain constant throughout your lifetime. Knowing what they are will help you understand how you operate in the world and how you differ from others with dissimilar striving instincts. Acting with your instincts, you'll find that you have almost inexhaustible energy, whereas acting against them, your energy is depleted quickly. The report you receive after completing the questionnaire will identify your instinctive talent and tell you how to put it to its best use. It will also provide you with some specific words that describe how you get things done when you're free to be yourself. This extra perspective can be very helpful in your efforts to identify patterns in the responses to your Unique Ability Question. It's highly likely that you'll see some connection between your instinctive creativity as identified by Kolbe and what people see as your Unique Ability. Since using your Unique Ability gives you energy, as does working with your instincts, it's likely that the two are linked. However, it's worthwhile to note that passion, which is another source of the energy you get from using your Unique Ability, comes from the affective part of the brain, and so is not part of your conative instincts. When the two act in concert, however, it's no surprise that you feel your Unique Ability is actually generating more energy than it's using up.

StrengthsFinder**.

The StrengthsFinder profile is presented in the book, *Now, Discover Your Strengths* by Marcus Buckingham and Donald O. Clifton. The book identifies a set of 34 possible strengths that the authors and the team at Gallup** identified during their research over a 25-year period. By doing a profile online, which you can access through a special code you get when you buy the book, you can learn what your top five strengths are. Highly engaging, articulate descriptions of each strength are provided in the book, along with examples of how that strength has actually been used to create positive results by real people. The words and phrases used in these descriptions are great material for articulating or clarifying aspects of your Unique Ability.

More information on these two tools and how to access them is located in the Appendix at the back of this book. Though a small monetary investment is required, we strongly suggest you give yourself the benefit of understanding your Kolbe A result and your StrengthsFinder profile. They're incredibly useful

---

*   The Kolbe A™ Index is a trademark of Kathy Kolbe. Used with permission.
** StrengthsFinder® and Gallup® are registered trademarks of The Gallup Organization.
    Used with permission.

in helping give you the words to express who you are and how you do things. And they provide tremendously self-affirming insight into important aspects of your uniqueness and how you make your best contributions to the world. If you do take advantage of these two profiles, enter your results in your notebook and note any key words or phrases that are meaningful to you.

Step 2: The 10 Best Habits™

Your unique "habits."

Your "best habits," by our definition, are the things you always do automatically to produce your best results. You've developed these over the course of your lifetime. When we think of habits, the bad ones usually come to mind. However, on closer observation, we all have a complete set of habits, some good and some perhaps not so good, that govern our everyday actions. The "badness" or "goodness" of our habits is all relative to whether they work for or against the things we're committed to. In the spectrum of your good habits, you have a smaller set of "best habits." This is where you want to focus so you can magnify what's best about you. By taking what's unconscious and making it conscious, you can give your best actions room to grow and flourish. We'll now work on identifying your 10 Best Habits, which are an important part of your Unique Ability. They complete the picture of *how* you operate when you're working in your Unique Ability. Label the next part of your notebook "My 10 Best Habits."

From all your good habits, we're going to pick the top ten. These 10 Best Habits reflect your values: You do these things because they're important to you. Others recognize that you do these things and have likely acknowledged you for them in the past. These habits are not ideal behaviors you wish you had or think you should have; they're the actual set of working principles that show up in your life consistently. It's important to be honest with yourself about this.

The responses you received to your Unique Ability Question will help you define your best habits. The things people wrote in their letters are based on their experience of you and represent their interpretation and personal viewpoint. They may list characteristics that describe you, but there's a difference between what you're actually doing and other people's perception of what you're doing. Your job is to get to the root of these perceptions.

I always ....

To start, look back over the responses and at your analysis of the feedback you received. Choose a topic or theme that is particularly meaningful to you. For instance, let's imagine someone said, "You get things done," another letter said, "You're a fantastic go-to person," and another commented, "You're extremely dependable and reliable." Here's the key question: *What do I do that has people say these things about me?* The way you phrase a best habit is to begin with the words "I always ...." So, for this example, maybe your first best habit is simply, "I always take action." This habit will be something you consider very important. To you, it's the "right" way to operate. In fact, it may frustrate you when others don't act in this way. This is a clue that you've found a great habit, because it's meaningful, and you really care about it. Your 10 Best Habits tap into your passion and values.

A few notes on style. A habit can be written simply — in only a few words — or can include a lot of detail. Either is fine. Your habits will reflect how you normally express things and will sound like you. If you're getting stuck on words, be playful. Get something down on paper and then edit as you go along. Choose words that you would use in daily conversation. Don't worry about how they may sound to others. These are written for you. If you'd like to have someone walk through this exercise with you, it can be helpful to have a good listener and someone to talk through ideas with.

Using the same process, complete your list of the 10 Best Habits that describe how you get your best results. You may be able to come up with some of your best habits off the top of your head because you already know these things about yourself and how you work. For instance, you "always tell the truth," or you "always make things fun." These may be core principles that you're very familiar with. Keep going until you have ten. Then look at what might be missing when conveying a complete picture of how you always do things.

Be sure to check each habit as you write it down, asking yourself, "Do I always do this? Do I feel passionate about doing it this way?" Does it feel like it would be wrong to operate any other way? If so, you're probably on to a best habit. For each habit, you also need to test to be sure you do it consistently in all areas of your life. Think of examples of various situations. Do you really *always* do this? If you can't truthfully say you always do it, then it's probably an ideal behavior you aspire to or just do once in awhile, rather than an actual habit. If it is a true best habit, it's likely you've been doing it for years. You may even have childhood memories of how this habit shaped your life in some way. Or perhaps you can trace its evolution back to a time when you learned that this way of acting worked for you.

When you're finished, you'll have a set of personal groundrules that guide your everyday actions. Now test them out on some people who know you well. Ask if anything is missing. Check to see if they "sound like you." In our experience, a person's 10 Best Habits create a recognizable portrait of who they are. In many cases, we can remove the person's name, and friends, family members, or co-workers who know them well can identify the person just from the list of habits. A good group of people to test your list with is the group who responded to your Unique Ability Question. They may even be able to help you refine some of your habits to get at more precise ways of describing what you "always do."

Here are some examples to help you get an idea of what habits sound like:

Kara W. — Project Manager

MY 10 BEST HABITS

1. I ALWAYS ASSESS THE SITUATION AND FIGURE OUT MY BEST FIT.

2. I ALWAYS STRIVE FOR BALANCE.

3. I ALWAYS ANALYZE MY PHYSICAL ENVIRONMENT.

4. I ALWAYS AM TRUE TO MYSELF.

5. I ALWAYS LAUGH AT THINGS TO ENJOY LIFE.

6. I ALWAYS ORGANIZE MYSELF.

7. I ALWAYS LEARN BY TRYING.

8. I ALWAYS SEE THE END RESULT AND THINK IT THROUGH TO A PLAUSIBLE SOLUTION.

9. I ALWAYS CHOOSE MY COMMITMENTS CAREFULLY AND THEN FOLLOW THROUGH.

10. I ALWAYS INSIST ON QUALITY.

Lindy V. — Recording Artist

My 10 Best Habits

1. I ALWAYS HELP TO DEVELOP PEOPLE'S PASSIONS BY PROVIDING ENCOURAGEMENT, LOVE, AND PRAISE.

2. I ALWAYS MAKE PEOPLE LAUGH.

3. I ALWAYS STRIVE TO ACHIEVE THE HIGHEST QUALITY IN MY WORK.

4. I ALWAYS MAKE THE BEST OUT OF EVERY SITUATION.

5. I ALWAYS HUG PEOPLE.

6. I ALWAYS WORK TO IMPROVE MYSELF SO I CAN BETTER SERVE OTHERS.

7. I ALWAYS COME UP WITH CREATIVE IDEAS AND WAYS FOR OTHERS TO IMPROVE THEIR LIVES AND WORK.

8. I ALWAYS SURROUND MYSELF WITH PEOPLE WHO ARE SMARTER THAN I AM.

9. I ALWAYS BELIEVE IN MYSELF AND HAVE CONFIDENCE THAT MY ACTIONS ARE WELL-INTENDED.

10. I ALWAYS TRY TO LIVE IN THE MOMENT.

Ben L. — Accountant

MY 10 BEST HABITS

1. I ALWAYS PUT MYSELF IN THE OTHER PERSON'S SHOES AND SEE WHAT THEY NEED.

2. I ALWAYS EMPOWER PEOPLE TO SOLVE PROBLEMS.

3. I ALWAYS CONNECT WITH PEOPLE.

4. I ALWAYS STAY CALM IN A DIFFICULT SITUATION.

5. I ALWAYS COMMUNICATE BY PERFORMING AND ENTERTAINING.

6. I ALWAYS MAKE PEOPLE FEEL COMFORTABLE.

7. I ALWAYS TRUST THAT THERE'S A SOLUTION OR A BETTER WAY.

8. I ALWAYS STICK TO MY BELIEFS AND VALUES.

9. I ALWAYS HAVE FUN.

10. I ALWAYS ADAPT MYSELF IN A SITUATION TO AVOID CONFLICT AND PROMOTE HARMONY.

Laurel K. — Program Consultant

MY 10 BEST HABITS

1. I ALWAYS LISTEN INTENTLY WITH A FOCUSED PRESENCE.

2. I ALWAYS ASK QUESTIONS TO UNDERSTAND AND CLARIFY.

3. I ALWAYS SHARE MY OBSERVATIONS AND PROVIDE A DIFFERENT PERSPECTIVE.

4. I ALWAYS SEE A CLEAR PATH THROUGH COMPLEXITY.

5. I ALWAYS USE METAPHORS AND ANALOGIES TO COMMUNICATE AN IDEA.

6. I ALWAYS ACKNOWLEDGE PEOPLE FOR WHO THEY ARE AND COMMUNICATE IN AN INDIVIDUALIZED WAY.

7. I ALWAYS AM EMPATHETIC AND CAN UNDERSTAND PEOPLE'S PERSPECTIVES IN A NON-JUDGMENTAL WAY.

8. I ALWAYS LOOK FOR WAYS TO IMPROVE THINGS.

9. I ALWAYS TAKE DECISIVE ACTION AND LEARN FROM THE RESULT.

10. I ALWAYS EXPRESS MY APPRECIATION.

Step 3: The Unique Ability Statement™

Distilling the essence.

By now, you have a lot of material to work with. It's time to extract your Unique Ability Statement — one sentence that expresses your Unique Ability. Here are some guidelines to help you as you look through the material you've collected:

- Unique Ability is the essence of what you love to do and do best, in all areas of your life.
- It is characterized by superior ability, passion, energy, and never-ending improvement.
- It can be applied to many different situations, activities, and opportunities.
- It's "factory installed" — you've been doing it since you were young.
- It may not seem exciting or special to you because it comes so naturally.
- Others may recognize it in you before you see it yourself.
- It evolves throughout your life and keeps getting better the more you apply it.

Defining your uniqueness.

Finding just the right words and the way they fit together to articulate your Unique Ability can be challenging and may take several drafts. Don't get discouraged. It's not always easy to be objective about something so close to you. Also, your Unique Ability is beyond words — the statement is simply a way to describe this fundamental aspect of who you are. You might spend a lot of time refining your Unique Ability Statement before you finally get something that feels exactly right. Expect that it will evolve over time as your understanding of your Unique Ability grows. But realize that even the earliest draft of your sentence will be light years away from what most people have to work with: People generally don't think about themselves as unique, let alone try to define their uniqueness. As you test your statement out in the world, you'll find yourself honing it, getting clearer and clearer about the nature of your Unique Ability and how to articulate it. Now it's time to create your statement.

My Unique Ability = Talent (what I do) + Passion (why I do it)

The formula.

The formula for creating a Unique Ability Statement is as follows: It starts with the words "My Unique Ability is ..." followed by action words that describe what you do (your talent), and then words that describe why you do it (your passion). Write this formula at the top of a new page in your notebook titled "My Unique Ability Statement."

Key words.

The first step is to collect some key words from all the work you've done so far. Look through the answers to your Unique Ability Question, at your list of 10 Best Habits, at any other profiles you may have completed (e.g. Kolbe, StrengthsFinder). List any words you think are important in describing your talent and passion. More is better — you may not use them all, but it's better to have lots to draw from.

Once you have your list of key words, you're going to start drafting your sentence. Start with the first part — what you do. There's something at the heart of all of the activities you're really good at and love doing. You're looking for the theme, the essence, the pattern behind your actions. This may not be obvious right away. The basic question here is "What?" What are you doing? What are you providing?

This statement is, first and foremost, for you, so don't worry about it being poetic or impressive. Its force isn't in the phrasing, but in its ability to make you say, "Yes, that is me. That really *is* what I do! I love doing that." Look for action words (verbs) that get to the heart of your superior abilities, like "explaining," "connecting," "strategizing," or "creating." Look at your list of key words and see what fits. For instance, Laurel recognized in her Unique Ability letters and her past experiences a common theme of communication, so she started her statement with, "My Unique Ability is communicating . . . ." Upon further reflection, she realized this was too vague. When she thought about what she actually loves about what she does in her job, and with her friends and family, she realized that she loves having conversations. That had a familiar ring. She recalled people really appreciating these "talks" and the insights and clarity they'd gained, so it seemed to be a superior ability. She was getting a bit closer. She thought about it more and talked it over with a few people, and realized that she isn't interested in having just any kind of conversation: They have to be meaningful and serve a purpose. In response, she refined the first part of her statement to say, "My Unique Ability is having purposeful conversations . . ." When she had that phrase, she knew she'd accurately described the essence of her natural talent.

As with your 10 Best Habits, it's important to get something down on paper to let your brain engage in the process. For many people, there are multiple dimensions to what they're doing. For example, "My Unique Ability is analyzing the details and creating logical, focused systems . . ." Analyzing details and creating systems are both integral parts of this Unique Ability. Here are other examples of the "talent" part of a few people's Unique Ability Statements:

My Unique Ability is connecting with people in a fun and lively way ...
My Unique Ability is figuring out a future vision and creating a flexible plan that can be implemented today ...
My Unique Ability is empathizing with people's individual experiences and taking action ...
My Unique Ability is communicating and responding with energy ...

*My Unique Ability is perceiving the essence of a situation
and providing practical strategies ...
My Unique Ability is connecting people to their wisdom ...
My Unique Ability is making authentic and enthusiastic connections...*

Notice that these actions are quite general. They have to be, in order to encompass the many circumstances in which you may use your Unique Ability. Unique Ability at its essence is not an activity or profession. Your Unique Ability is not "selling" or "writing." These verbs are too specific to apply to a variety of situations. You will see later that things like writing and selling are "Unique Ability Activities" — part of the set of activities and situations that allow you to express your Unique Ability.

Now move on to the second part of your sentence. The basic question here is "Why?" Why do you do this? What's your motivation? Why do you bother? What result are you hoping to achieve? What are you really committed to? This part of your statement describes your passion and what you really value. Sometimes this part of the sentence is easier to come up with than the description of what you're doing.

Here are some examples of the second part of some statements:

*... to empower them to be confident in themselves and experience the joy
of new possibilities.
... to achieve the best results.
... so they feel cared for.
... to achieve an improved result.
... to align people's thinking with what's real.
... to transform their future.
... to motivate people to have fun and make improvements to lead a
happier life.*

Put these two parts together, the "what" and the "why," and you've got a basic first draft of your Unique Ability Statement.

My Unique Ability® is ...

Talent (what I do) + Passion (why I do it)	
Ben L.	"My Unique Ability is connecting with people in a fun and lively way to empower them to be confident in themselves and experience the joy of new possibilities."
Tami C.	"My Unique Ability is figuring out a future vision and creating a flexible plan that can be implemented today to achieve the best results."
Erin S.	"My Unique Ability is empathizing with people's individual experiences and taking action so they feel cared for."
Ross S.	"My Unique Ability is communicating and responding with energy to achieve an improved result."
Shannon W.	"My Unique Ability is perceiving the essence of a situation and providing practical strategies to align people's thinking with what's real."
Cheryl D.	"My Unique Ability is connecting people to their wisdom to transform their future."
Katherine E.	"My Unique Ability is making authentic and enthusiastic connections to motivate people to have fun and make improvements to lead a happier life."

Congratulations on getting this far. You've done the hardest part. The next step is all about editing and playing with words to come up with something that feels right. (Many of the examples you've just read were developed and crafted over a period of weeks or months.) Read your sentence out loud. Go through it word by word and see what fits and what doesn't. Use a thesaurus to help you find words that express your ideas in the best way. Try rearranging words — it can make a big difference. Read your statement to others who know you well to see what needs refining. At this point, you may want to add some descriptive words to complete the picture and personalize it more. These can help describe how you do what you do.

Editing Tips:
- Read aloud to others
- Rearrange
- Use a thesaurus
- Add descriptive words

It's important to test your sentence to be sure it applies to all the situations in your life where you use your Unique Ability. For example, it shouldn't only fit for your work or school activities; it also needs to apply at home, with friends and family, and in the daily activities where you exhibit a superior ability and passion. Here are a couple of examples of how an effective statement captures a variety of activities.

Myrna N.'s Unique Ability is "finessing and organizing every detail to create an enjoyable experience that is both impeccable and harmonious." At work, she applies this to her job as a writer, editor, and proofreader. In the editing and proofreading process, her goal is to produce a piece that is clear, concise, and easy to read. As the last "pair of eyes" to see everything before it is sent out to print, she pores over every word and comma, making sure everything's in the right place to create as perfect a piece as possible. Myrna's Unique Ability is not just evident in her work life. At home, her Unique Ability comes out in her passion for cooking, entertaining, decorating, and gardening. In her cooking, not only taste, but color, texture, and presentation are essential ingredients. But as much as she loves the cooking process itself, creating a beautiful experience for her guests is her main motivation — even if those "guests" are her two teenaged children. Myrna's unerring eye for detail is also reflected in her garden and in her home's charming décor. Another reflection of her Unique Ability is her dedication to creating a stable and harmonious home for her two children. Myrna can also see her Unique Ability in action in such everyday activities as doing laundry, writing an "organized" grocery list, and choosing and wrapping a "just right" gift. Friends and family members are always delighted to be on her guest and gift lists — and are rarely disappointed.

Perry G.'s Unique Ability is "to identify what is missing or needed — and, in the moment, synergistically combine energy and resources — to proactively create a new, better reality." In all parts of his life, Perry seems to be unaffected by the mental barriers that hold most people back. By following his passion, he has rapidly and repeatedly established and reinvented himself in ways that have astonished, inspired, and created value for others. As a teenager, he opened Toronto's first indoor skateboard park and built an international skateboard brand, creating the opportunity for many young Canadian athletes to participate in the California-dominated industry. Then, recognizing an opportunity for Canadian influence in the emerging snowboard business, he founded a multi-million-dollar snowboard company. Currently, Perry combines his passion for adventure and business acumen as a producer and director of music videos, commercials, and radio documentaries. His Unique Ability has made him a respected advisor and consultant on several boards and to a wide variety of organizations in different industries. In his personal life, his ability to conjure up magic in the moment is used to create memorable, unique experiences for his friends and family, and especially for his nieces, who adore him.

On a fresh page in your notebook, take a moment to rewrite your Unique Ability Statement followed by your 10 Best Habits. This page should now articulate fairly well who you are, what you do best, and how you operate. If you were to share this with others, it alone would give people a very good idea of what they could expect from you and count on you for.

MY UNIQUE ABILITY   BEN

MY UNIQUE ABILITY IS CONNECTING WITH PEOPLE IN A FUN AND
LIVELY WAY TO EMPOWER THEM TO BE CONFIDENT IN THEM-
SELVES AND EXPERIENCE THE JOY OF NEW POSSIBILITIES.

MY 10 BEST HABITS

1. I ALWAYS PUT MYSELF IN THE OTHER PERSON'S
   SHOES AND SEE WHAT THEY NEED.

2. I ALWAYS EMPOWER PEOPLE TO SOLVE PROBLEMS.

3. I ALWAYS CONNECT WITH PEOPLE.

4. I ALWAYS STAY CALM IN A DIFFICULT SITUATION.

5. I ALWAYS COMMUNICATE BY PERFORMING
   AND ENTERTAINING.

6. I ALWAYS MAKE PEOPLE FEEL COMFORTABLE.

7. I ALWAYS TRUST THAT THERE'S A SOLUTION OR A
   BETTER WAY.

8. I ALWAYS STICK TO MY BELIEFS AND VALUES.

9. I ALWAYS HAVE FUN.

10. I ALWAYS ADAPT MYSELF IN A SITUATION TO AVOID
    CONFLICT AND PROMOTE HARMONY.

Now that you've done this thinking, how do you feel? John Hittler had this to say:

After defining my Unique Ability, I noticed that there were several phases that I went through. It started with 'is that all it is?' since it seemed like what I could do was so easy. I simply did not realize that the rest of the world could not do that.

After that it took a while to begin to 'own' my Unique Ability, in that I knew what I could do, but I was hesitant to test it thoroughly. What if it really didn't hold true? What if I got in over my head?

As time passed, and I realized that the more challenges to the Unique Ability, the better it became, and the more I liked it, I started to plan for opportunities to utilize the Unique Ability. This simply took awhile.

Now that I set up life in a large part to take full advantage of my Unique Ability, I stay out of areas where I have no business playing, and get involved in areas where I might previously have stayed away. I can make a big difference where I choose, and avoid the hassles and stress of getting involved with areas that are a conflict — that is, where my Unique Ability is not needed or utilized.

John Hittler

Here's what some other people said about how it feels to be able to articulate your Unique Ability clearly:

Knowing more about my Unique Ability and having greater clarity allows the extraneous and doubt to fall away leaving the 'pure' of who I am to be brought into greater focus.

Jim M.

It is my yard stick for what I should be involved in and what I shouldn't be involved in. It allows me to give people a quick idea about what I do that creates value.

Gaynor R.

This sounds silly, but I feel emotionally organized. When I question something I'm doing I can now go back to my statement and perhaps better understand my motives ... it justifies what I've been calling my intuition.

Erin S.

It makes me feel very confident about what I should be focusing my energies on — and what I shouldn't.

Myrna N.

It feels awesome. I feel like I discovered a part of myself I never knew how to articulate to others.

Tami C.

To better understand how all the pieces of The Unique Ability Discovery Process work together to define a person's Unique Ability, refer to Kara W.'s example under "Anatomy of a Unique Ability" in the Appendix.

The benefits of sharing.
One thing you can do immediately with your Unique Ability statement is to share it with the key people in your life.

Opening up opportunities.
Your Unique Ability, however precisely you've been able to define it, gives you a way to articulate what you're naturally good at to other people. Once others

understand your Unique Ability, they can help you find opportunities to use it, and they can tap into it themselves. You'll be the person they think of when they, or someone else they know, need someone with your talent and passion. As you worked through these first steps of The Unique Ability Discovery Process, you may already have had some ideas about how it would be useful to share your insights with others. Some people we know have said they'd like to put it on their resumes or post it on their office doors. Some said they were happy to have an easy way to quickly explain what they do that creates value, particularly people whose job titles only vaguely capture what they actually do.

Giving others direction.

Clearly articulating what you love to do will increase the likelihood that when opportunities and referrals come your way, they'll be things you'll actually want to do rather than things someone else thought you'd be good at but you're not really that excited about. As you've seen if you've done The Unique Ability Question exercise, other people perceive your Unique Ability from the point of view of the value it creates for them. Only you can say what really gives you energy. For example, someone might say, "You're a great cook, and whatever you make is always different and delicious." Perhaps you love finding new recipes and have a skill for sourcing really good ones and executing them superbly. On the other hand, maybe you're a talented innovator who has an innate understanding of ingredients and the basic principles of cooking and loves to create brilliant dishes in the moment without using recipes at all. In the first case, you might love a gift of the hottest new cookbook, or be thrilled to help when someone is planning a dinner party and having difficulty figuring out the menu. However, if you're actually the improviser who never uses a recipe, you may not really appreciate the cookbook, and the dinner party queries could stress you out. What might really get you excited, though, is a friend calling you in a panic because they have nothing in their pantry but tinned fish, beans, and some condiments, and they need to make something edible for unexpected guests — exactly what would stress out the great recipe-finder. Often, the only way people know what lies behind the results they identify with your Unique Ability is if you tell them. Giving them this information actually provides them with valuable direction about how to engage your passion for your benefit and theirs.

Grow your Unique Ability resource pool.

Sharing your Unique Ability will help keep your project of pursuing it alive and moving forward. Another by-product is the excitement and enthusiasm you spark in others. Unique Ability is a concept with a strong emotional pull. Those who hear about it tend to be eager to learn more and are naturally curious about what theirs might be. If you help someone else discover their Unique Ability, you'll benefit not only from assisting them, but from getting clearer about their Unique Ability and how it might be useful to you or others you know.

Step 4: The Activity Inventory™

A cross-section of your life.

Your Unique Ability is expressed through a variety of activities in your life. It's time to take a closer look at what you spend your time doing and how much opportunity you have to apply your Unique Ability.

The positive feedback, enjoyment, and energy you get back from activities that utilize your Unique Ability make you want to do them more and get even better at them. Nonetheless, we all do many things every day that don't engage our Unique Ability. These next steps will help you to identify which activities use your Unique Ability and distinguish them from everything else you do. From there, it becomes possible to create strategies to do more of what you're "unique" at and less of everything else.

The Activity Inventory allows you to create a comprehensive summary of all the activities in your life so you can analyze them. This exercise is designed to capture as many of your daily activities as possible, like taking a cross-section of your life. Label the next page in your notebook "My Activity Inventory." Start by making a list of the things you do in the course of your routine, both at work and in your personal life. Look at the "micro" scale of your activities — daily tasks like organizing your schedule, having phone conversations, answering e-mail, making meals, family duties, and the particulars of your day at home, at school, or at work. Try to get at a fairly broad list of examples, but don't get too carried away. Brushing your teeth and other daily necessities need not be included.

Come up with as many things as you can as they occur to you. Imagine a day, from the time you wake up in the morning to the time you go to bed — for both weekdays and weekends — and chronicle as many of your activities as possible. Next, expand your scope to a month or a year. Perhaps there are bigger projects you've worked on in the past or which lie ahead that belong on your list. Don't worry about writing them in any order; it doesn't matter. The example on the following page will give you an idea of what to include.

You may want to carry your Inventory around with you for a week, since you likely do lots of things that you might not think of including at first. If you get stuck, show someone else your list and ask him or her to help you fill in what's missing. The more of your life you can capture now, the more useful your list will be later.

If there are any activities that you're new at, or have very little experience with, leave them off your list for now. It's probably too soon to accurately judge your feelings or results in these areas, which will make them difficult to categorize in the next step.

MY ACTIVITY INVENTORY

WORK	HOME
FOLLOW-UP EMAILS	MANAGING FINANCES
CLIENT CORRESPONDENCE	PAYING BILLS
INTERNET RESEARCH	FIXING THINGS AROUND THE HOUSE
WRITING STATUS REPORTS	ERRANDS
SCHEDULING APPOINTMENTS	YARD WORK
COORDINATING TEAM MEMBERS	KEEPING IN TOUCH W/ FRIENDS
GIVING PRESENTATIONS	CLEANING OUT THE GARAGE
TEAM STRATEGY MEETINGS	LEADING CHARITY MEETINGS
SOLVING CLIENT PROBLEMS	HOSTING DINNER PARTIES
BUSINESS READING	COORDINATING FAMILY EVENTS
MANAGING GREENWOOD PROJECT	PLANNING VACATIONS
TRAINING NEW HIRES	GROCERY SHOPPING
REGULAR CLIENT MEETINGS	READING FOR PLEASURE
FILING	READING TO THE KIDS
TRACKING BILLABLE TIME & INVOICING	HELPING KIDS W/ HOMEWORK
ORGANIZING MY PROJECTS	PREPARING MEALS
PLANNING MY TIME	EXERCISING

The four types of activities.

Your Unique Ability doesn't show up in a vacuum. By looking at your whole life and identifying which activities engage it, you can see what other demands might be getting in its way. We'll begin by establishing four categories of activities — Unique, Excellent, Competent, and Incompetent. Everything you do can be categorized this way.

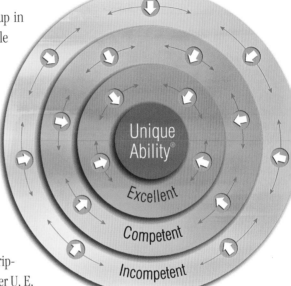

After reading the following descriptions, you're going to place the letter U, E, C, or I — representing the appropriate category — beside each activity on your Activity Inventory list. Here are the descriptions of each category:

Unique Ability Activities.

• **Superior skill** • **Energy** • **Passion** • **Never-ending improvement**
Of the activities on your list, which ones are your favorites, the ones you love to do? Others agree that you show superior skill in these areas. These activities create more energy than they use up. When you're engaged in them, you lose track of time. As a test: Could you do this all day long and still keep going? If it's part of your job, would you still want to do it even if you didn't get paid for it? If you've received any training or instruction in this area, you were probably a star student because you've got a natural ability here. There are always new and exciting possibilities for improvement, no matter how good you get.

Excellent Activities.
• Superior skill • Reputation • No passion • Teamwork
Of your activities, which do you recognize as something you do better than
most people? You've got a superior skill in this area, so you find these activities satisfying, and you find the results you can create rewarding. People count
on you for what you're able to do in this area. You may have developed a reputation for your ability. Many people may want you to work with or for them,
and they provide you with opportunities to do these things. There's a great
sense of teamwork: People want to work with you because your abilities meet
the highest standards. But deep down, you don't have a real sense of passion
for the activity. In fact, you may not even like to do it. For all the external plus-
es, these activities don't tap into your internal motivations. This lack of passion is what differentiates excellent from Unique Ability activities.

Competent Activities.
• Meet minimum standards • Anxiety • Competition • Repetition
There are other activities on your list that you're merely adequate at — you
reach minimum standards. You're simply okay, and a lot of others could do
these activities with much greater success or a lot less effort. Because you aren't
distinct from others, you face a lot of competition. You may worry about
falling behind, failing, or becoming obsolete. The activity seems the same, day
after day, which leads to boredom. You don't feel particularly inspired to get
better, and your efforts don't bring you any kind of growth. There is little or no
improvement in your performance over time.

Incompetent Activities.
• Failure • Frustration • Conflict • Stress
It's often very clear where your Unique Ability isn't. Which activities on your list
make you feel frustrated or stressed because you're just not good at them? Which
activities would you be happy never to do again? You might have put a lot of time

and effort into these, but you still don't get a good result. Nothing seems to work, and you can't make headway. If you were going to be good at them, you would be by now — but it's just not happening. You might also find yourself in conflict with others when you're doing these things because of your low skill level. Breakdowns in communication occur frequently. Everything is difficult.

A word on "hobbies."

Occasionally, someone will come across an activity that they love to do but are basically competent or incompetent at. Some of our clients have put activities like golf in this category. Though they may not be great golfers, they do get enjoyment from being out on the course, from the social aspects of the game, and from the relief it gives them from their busy lives. If you find that you have an item like this on your list, you may want to redefine it to break it down into its component parts and try categorizing those. However, if skill really isn't an issue, either because the activity requires no skill or because you don't strive to develop your capabilities since it's a hobby that you do for other reasons, this activity may not be a useful addition to your list.

Categorize your activities.

Go through your Activity Inventory list now, and categorize your activities according to the descriptions above. Mark each item as follows:

U for Unique Ability activities.
E for Excellent activities.
C for Competent activities.
I for Incompetent activities.

It's important to tell the truth about your ability level or lack thereof. You don't need to be good at everything. Operating in a Unique Ability framework means finding ways to let go of what you're not good at. Give yourself permission to

MY ACTIVITY INVENTORY

WORK

FOLLOW-UP EMAILS	C
CLIENT CORRESPONDENCE	E
INTERNET RESEARCH	U
WRITING STATUS REPORTS	E
SCHEDULING APPOINTMENTS	C
COORDINATING TEAM MEMBERS	E
GIVING PRESENTATIONS	U
TEAM STRATEGY MEETINGS	E
SOLVING CLIENT PROBLEMS	U
BUSINESS READING	E
MANAGING GREENWOOD PROJECT	U
TRAINING NEW HIRES	I
REGULAR CLIENT MEETINGS	U
FILING	C
TRACKING BILLABLE TIME & INVOICING	C
ORGANIZING MY PROJECTS	E
PLANNING MY TIME	E

HOME

MANAGING FINANCES	E
PAYING BILLS	C
FIXING THINGS AROUND THE HOUSE	I
ERRANDS	C
YARD WORK	C
KEEPING IN TOUCH W/ FRIENDS	I
CLEANING OUT THE GARAGE	I
LEADING CHARITY MEETINGS	U
HOSTING DINNER PARTIES	U
COORDINATING FAMILY EVENTS	C
PLANNING VACATIONS	C
GROCERY SHOPPING	C
READING FOR PLEASURE	U
READING TO THE KIDS	U
HELPING KIDS W/ HOMEWORK	C
PREPARING MEALS	I
EXERCISING	I

delegate things that are not your Unique Ability, but understand that labeling something an incompetent or competent activity is not an excuse for being irresponsible about your commitments.

Step 5: The Activity Snapshot™

Now that you've categorized your activities, it's time to reorganize and rewrite them by category so you can clearly see all of your areas of Unique Ability, excellence, competence, and incompetence. This will help you to look at a situation and recognize in advance where your efforts will be effective and where you'll probably find yourself frustrated.

In order to best organize your information, divide the next page of your notebook into four quadrants and title it "My Activity Snapshot." In each of the four boxes, write one of the four types of ability — Unique, Excellent, Competent, or Incompetent. Now choose a category to start with, for example, incompetent, and find all the activities you have labeled with an "I." Study them, grouping similar activities. Give each grouping an overall name and enter it in in your Snapshot. For instance, if the incompetent activities on your Inventory include "fixing the toaster," "unjamming the photocopier," and "figuring out what's wrong with the car," you might say on your Snapshot that you're incompetent at "mechanical work." External, physical activities such as these will probably be easy to group together. For some other types of activities, it may be more difficult to identify the common element; for instance, activities in which you're interacting with others, like "relationship building," or making use of your inner resources, such as "problem solving" or "investigating alternatives." Cross each activity off your Activity Inventory as you group them so you don't get confused. Be sure to include them all.

MY ACTIVITY SNAPSHOT

UNIQUE	EXCELLENT
RESEARCHING	WRITING
MANAGING PROJECTS	MANAGING MONEY
CLIENT COMMUNICATION	TEAM MANAGEMENT
PROBLEM SOLVING	RESEARCH
HOSTING EVENTS	

COMPETENT	INCOMPETENT
ROUTINE ACTIVITIES	ANYTHING MECHANICAL
SCHEDULING	CLEANING
ADMINISTRATION/	TRAINING
PAPERWORK	PREPARING MEALS
	EXERCISING

Having a simple overview of the activities for which you have a particular strength or weakness will give you the clarity to avoid situations that waste your time and to spend more of your life doing what you love to do.

Step 6: The Unique Ability Action Plan™

Now let's look at your Activity Snapshot to see what you can do differently to free up your energy. How can you do less of your incompetent or merely competent activities? These are usually the areas to target first. They're the "red alert" areas that if unattended could lead to failure or conflict. The time and energy that's freed up allows you to concentrate more on your excellent and Unique Ability activities.

Create a simple action plan for yourself.

Divide a notebook page into four columns and title it "My Unique Ability Action Plan." Across the top, label the columns: Improvement Ideas, Benefits, Specific Actions, and Deadline Dates.

Improvement Ideas.

Under Improvement Ideas, write down the changes you could make to eliminate non-Unique Ability activities and free you up to spend more time working in your Unique Ability.

The first thing to do is to take a look at everything on the bottom half of your Activity Snapshot page — the competent and incompetent sections. Figuring out how to stop doing everything in the incompetent section is the most urgent. You may feel as though you should get better at these things, but, truthfully, the amount of time, energy, money, and other people's investment it would take to improve isn't worth it. Your resources will be much better put to use supporting the growth and development of your Unique Ability.

How do you stop doing your incompetent activities? It depends on the situation. If it's not really that important, you may be able to just stop doing it without any negative consequences. You can delegate the activity if you've got someone available to do it. Another option is to trade this activity with someone else, in exchange for something you'd rather do and they'd rather not. Sometimes, using technology to automate an activity can get it off your plate. Can you pay someone else to do it for you ? This often doesn't cost a lot. If you feel guilty about passing off the tasks you hate, think about it this way: You're giving someone else who likes this activity the opportunity to do more of it and possibly even get paid for doing it. Give yourself permission to delegate, knowing that you and the rest of the world are generally better off when you get rid of incompetent activities in favor of your Unique Ability. Next, look at how to apply the same strategies to your competent activities.

Delegation Strategies:
- Stop doing it.
- Find someone else to do it.
- Trade with someone else.
- Use technology.
- Hire someone.
- Give up guilt.

You'll engage your creativity much faster if you move beyond the emotional roadblocks to focusing on your Unique Ability. Our culture is very much one of "rugged individualism," with the mindset, "I can do it better myself." This has evolved to, "I *should* be able to do everything myself, better than anyone else." Needless to say, it's not possible, practical, or desirable to function this way, but a little voice in our head often preaches this impossible standard.

Ultimately, you even want to eliminate excellent activities. This advice surprises people, but often the thing holding a person back from extraordinary achievements is their clinging to what's merely really good. Plain and simple, excellent activities can take up a lot of time. You may get praised and rewarded well for doing them because you're really talented and you produce great results, so the temptation is strong to keep doing them. They're safe, even if they're not particularly exciting or inspiring. Still, your efforts would be better invested in Unique Ability activities, where, paradoxically, you have the greatest room for improvement. Unique Ability is an area where you can keep having breakthroughs, feeling excited, and creating valuable results long past the point where others lose steam. Your Unique Ability is an endlessly renewable resource. If you want to keep increasing the size of your contribution and the impact of your talents, you may eventually need to create room by getting rid of some of your excellent activities. This doesn't have to happen overnight or all at once; nevertheless, it may feel like a leap of faith at first.

Getting rid of non-Unique Ability activities allows you to disengage your mind and emotions from things that don't really get you excited and may even drain your energy. This makes more time and mental energy available to devote to doing those things you love. To take full advantage of these reclaimed personal resources, you need to make a commitment and proactively plan to use the time and energy you gain to focus more on your Unique Ability. Look at your Unique Ability activities. What needs to happen for you to expand the time you spend on them or increase the value you create with them? These are important items to add to your list of improvement ideas. See the example on page 63 for ideas.

An investment, not a cost.
Ideally, the rewards from making the improvements you've listed should more than make up for any expenses associated with them. Any money you use to hire someone or buy technology to get rid of a non-Unique Ability activity should be considered an investment, not a cost. It's an investment in the future growth of your Unique Ability, which should pay large dividends. See our example for ideas.

As you brainstorm possible improvements, be open-minded. Even slight changes can be tremendously rewarding, as you find yourself free of a task you always hated doing, or find that what you most love to do really is valuable to other people. We often labor needlessly, for whatever reason, under the idea that things can't be this easy. Imagine that they can be. Lots of people get to do what they love and get paid for it because they've worked out the fit between their abilities and the world's needs. You can do this, too. It may be a lifelong process, but it's well worth pursuing.

Benefits.

To motivate yourself to take action, describe the benefit of making each improvement. Under Benefits, write how each improvement could make things better. Would this free your time? Prevent frustration? Create work for someone else? Would this improvement give your talent new outlets?

Specific actions.

Under Specific Actions, list the specific things you can do to make each improvement idea a reality. Use action words and phrases like "call," "meet with," "strategize," "talk to," "ask," and so on.

Deadline dates.

In this column, enter a "by when" date for making this improvement. Having a completion date helps focus your thinking. If you use an organizer, you may want to copy the deadlines for your various improvements into your calendar. You might want to list the specific people you need to contact, too.

A balance test.

Some people find, as they examine their lists, that most of the activities they're unique at happen in one part of their life, for example, at work as opposed to at home. If this is your situation, you most likely enjoy spending time working,

My Unique Ability Action Plan

	IMPROVEMENT IDEAS	BENEFITS	SPECIFIC ACTIONS	DEADLINE DATES
1.	HIRE YARD SERVICE	WON'T HAVE TO WORRY ABOUT IT	ASK JOE FOR REFERRAL	2 WEEKS
2.	ASK CHRIS TO TAKE OVER TRAINING	WON'T HAVE TO DO IT ANYMORE	SET UP MEETING WITH CHRIS & JAMIE	NEXT WEEK
3.	SIGN UP FOR EXERCISE CLASS	A REGULAR CLASS WILL PROVIDE SOME STRUCTURE	CHECK OUT NEW YOGA STUDIO	2 WEEKS
4.	HIRE A BOOK-KEEPER	FREED UP TO FOCUS ON PLANNING	ADVERTISE IN LOCAL PAPER	6 WEEKS
5.	BUY SCHEDUL-ING SOFTWARE	WILL MAKE IT FASTER & EASIER	RESEARCH ON THE NET	1 MONTH
6.	HOST MAJOR FUNDRAISER	RAISE LOTS OF MONEY, FUN TO DO	BRING UP AT NEXT COMMIT-TEE MEETING	NEXT YEAR

and derive a lot of emotional satisfaction from it. If you spend a lot of time at home doing your incompetent activities, it's easy to begin to feel that you don't have much of a personal life. The difference in the feeling you get at work and at home can be a motivation to become a workaholic at the expense of the rest of your life. Conversely, your current work pursuits may not engage your Unique Ability, whereas you do get to use your talents in your personal life. This can leave you looking at the clock, waiting for it to signal the end of the day. Either way, some part of your life is not giving you the satisfaction it could be, a situation which can lead to other problems and conflicts. Here are some ideas to encourage a better balance: Look back at your Unique Ability Statement and find ways to apply it more in the area of your life where it's being neglected. You may be able to change your role at work to one that takes advantage of your Unique Ability. If you're using your Unique Ability at home, look to see if there's an opportunity somehow to make money doing these activities for others. By taking a fresh look at how you contribute, you can be happier and create enormous value for others.

Unique Ability Growth Strategies:
- Give yourself permission to spend time using your Unique Ability.
- Talk to as many people as possible about it. Get the word out.
- Seek new opportunities and audiences.
- Ask others for support, suggestions, and ideas.
- Look for the resources you need to grow your Unique Ability.
- Put structures in your life that support the development of your Unique Ability.
- Make time for thinking, learning, and personal awareness.

Reshaping your life.

Any increase in the amount of time you spend using your Unique Ability will noticeably improve your life because you'll be replacing activities for which you have no passion with things that give you energy and generate great results. Once you get started, you'll find it easier to identify even more areas where you can do this. You'll develop a much stronger understanding of what your Unique Ability is and how it's best delivered to the world. These are things you can only learn through experience. Stripping away non-Unique Ability activities is the first step on this path. Michelangelo once said, "As the marble wastes, the statue grows." As the sculptor of your own life, you must systematically chisel away all the extra "marble" that obscures who you really are. As you do, the unique work of art your life can be will emerge with increasing clarity. Every layer of non-Unique Ability activity you remove gets you a little bit clearer on what your Unique Ability is and how to focus on it even more. The energy and benefits you get fuel this transformation and become powerful motivation to find ways to focus even more on what you love.

> As the sculptor of your own life, you must systematically chisel away all the extra "marble" that obscures who you really are.

The indispensible role of others.

Even though your Unique Ability is intrinsic to who you are as an individual, working with others is necessary to achieve the greatest results. The only way to effectively spend large amounts of time in your Unique Ability is to partner with others. Dan Sullivan, after 20 years of focusing on his Unique Ability, building structures and relationships to support it and constantly seeking to work more and more within it, estimates that he spends 95 percent of his work time on Unique Ability activities. His wife and business partner, Babs Smith, has been instrumental in helping him to continually strip away non-Unique Ability activities and in building the structures that allowed this to happen. Often it's other people's questions and actions that provoke you to spend more time doing your Unique Ability. Babs kept asking Dan, "Why are *you* doing this?" She would find other ways to get things done that were obviously not Unique Ability activities for Dan. This freed up Dan to focus on and develop his Unique Ability. Without Babs' vision of the bigger impact that Dan's ideas could have on the world and her ability to create a support system to leverage him, Dan might still be functioning as a "rugged individual," trying to do it all himself.

Even when Dan was still doing many things that were not his Unique Ability, the time he did spend focusing on it allowed their company to grow exponentially. There is a double benefit in that much of what Dan gave up was delegated to others who had Unique Abilities in those areas. Not only was his ability leveraged, other tasks were able to take on new life in the hands of people with passion and creativity in those areas. In this way, every percent that was delegated had an exponential return in terms of increased results.

John Hittler, whose story began this book, estimates that he currently spends 40 percent of his working time in his Unique Ability. This doesn't include time he spends in his personal life, where he uses his Unique Ability in many ways with his family and with charities, as well as in countless other interactions he has each day. Others we interviewed were thrilled to be spending even ten percent of their time in their businesses working on their Unique Ability. While every one of these people has a goal to increase that percentage, they all reported that they felt considerably liberated and energized by what they had already achieved.

Setting a goal.

Here's a quick thinking exercise. Estimate what percentage of time you spend using your Unique Ability in all areas of your life right now. This isn't a precise science, so don't worry if you can only come up with a very rough number. Now

MY UNIQUE ABILITY GOAL

ACTUAL: 5% NOVEMBER 1	GOAL: 50% JUNE 1

PROGRESS & NOTES:

NOV. 20   PASSED OFF TRAINING RESPONSIBILITIES TO CHRIS &
          JAMIE. FREED ME UP TO FOCUS ON TEAM STRATEGY
          MEETINGS & TO SPEND MORE TIME WITH CLIENTS.

DEC. 15   HIRED TIM NEXT DOOR TO DO REGULAR YARD WORK.
          HE ENJOYS IT A LOT MORE THAN I DO, AND I HAVE
          MORE TIME TO RELAX.

FEB. 21   HOSTED MAJOR CHARITY FUNDRAISER. RAISED MOST
          FUNDS IN ITS HISTORY AND GENERATED GREAT PUBLICITY.

think about what your life would be like if you could increase that number. If it's five percent now, how would your life be different if you could double it to ten percent? Remember, this means that not only will you be spending twice as much time doing what you love, you'll be getting rid of all the activities that aren't your Unique Ability which currently use up that time. Maybe you'd like to increase it even more.

Take a fresh page in your notebook and label it "My Unique Ability Goal." Then write "Actual" and "Goal." Beside Actual, write down the percentage you estimated for today with today's date. Next to it, beside Goal, write down your goal for how much time you'd like to be spending in your Unique Ability and a date by which you'd like to see that become a reality. Below, write "Progress and Notes" and make notes on your progress as you begin to make changes and implement your improvement ideas. This will be an experimental process. You may find that small changes make a big difference, or you may find that you have to do more than you initially thought. The important thing is to keep focused on moving forward from where you are now, learn as you go, and celebrate your achievements along the way, whether they're big or small. As we like to say in The Strategic Coach, it's about progress, not perfection.

By doing these exercises, you've laid the foundation for a bigger, better future. You've done a lot of work and hopefully learned a lot about yourself. You may be eager to get to the next stage — putting what you've learned to use. Or perhaps you've already begun to make changes and experience the impact. Either way, this is a great time to take a moment to acknowledge and celebrate your progress. You've already done more than most people ever do to clarify how you can make your best contribution to the world and to your own happiness. The next chapters will show you how to build on this foundation and use your Unique Ability as the basis to shape the life you want.

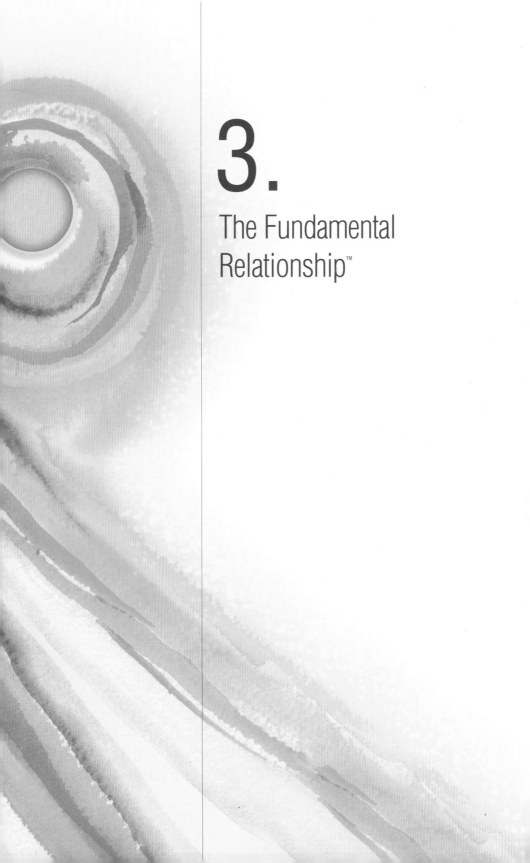

3.

The Fundamental
Relationship™

Unique Ability

Creating The Life You Want

Chapter 3:
The Fundamental Relationship™

*H*appiness and The Fundamental Relationship.

What now?

You've taken steps to discover your Unique Ability and to differentiate it from all the other things you do. Over time, you'll have insights that allow you to even more clearly understand and articulate what it is. With that very important part of the process under way, it's time to focus on how you can put this knowledge to work to improve the quality of your life.

> *The secret to a happy life is to discover what you love doing and develop a way of getting paid for it. A greater secret is to do what you love, get paid for it, and make a great contribution to other people. And the greatest secret of all is to do what you love, make a great contribution, and get extraordinarily well-paid for it.*
> **Dan Sullivan**

Take it to the world — strategically.

At this point, you may not be really clear about how your Unique Ability interacts with the world or how to use it to create the life you want. In order to make something work better, you first have to understand how it operates on a fundamental level. The following pages will introduce you to a model called "The Fundamental Relationship." This framework will give you a language and a structure to examine, analyze, and take charge of your most basic and

The Fundamental Relationship™

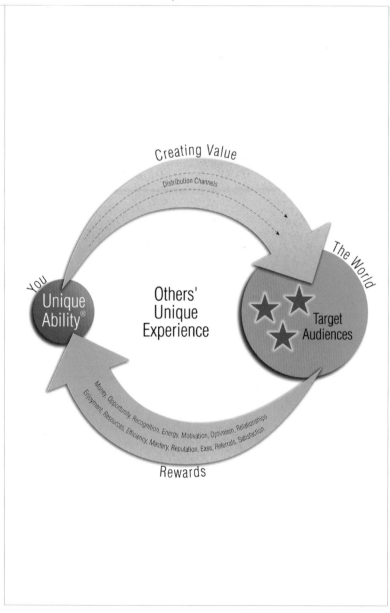

important relationship — the one that ultimately allows your unique talents and passion to make the greatest contribution and return to you the greatest quality of life. Understanding the nature of this relationship with the world and all its components will allow you to evolve and strengthen it consciously and strategically to create the future you want.

Understanding The Fundamental Relationship.

Your Unique Ability needs other people, and other people need your Unique Ability. The Fundamental Relationship describes how your Unique Ability and the world can interact most productively. As is true in any good relationship, each side gives, and each side receives. Several components link to form this circular relationship. These include your Unique Ability and others' experience of it; how you create value and through which "distribution channels" you deliver it; the audiences you target — for whom you create value; and the rewards and benefits you receive as a result of your value creation. In a nutshell, you use your Unique Ability to create value for specific groups of individuals in the world and they directly or indirectly reward you for that value. These rewards, in the form of money, recognition, resources, opportunities, and a host of other things we'll examine later, give you what you need to further develop your Unique Ability and create even more value. As you do this, you receive even greater rewards. This is the way the relationship builds to deliver you a greater and greater quality of life as you deliver increasing amounts of value to the world.

... your efforts have the force of your passion and your natural talents behind them.

Though the dynamic is simple, each component of the relationship is unique for every individual. You have a sense of the first part, which is your Unique Ability. Now we'll look at it, and each of the other pieces, so that you can see in detail how your own fundamental relationship currently operates and how you might like to evolve or strengthen parts of it. Along the way, we'll look at the example of Marilyn W., a member of The Strategic Coach team who has been developing her fundamental relationship, without being conscious of it in these terms, for more than 30 years.

You and your Unique Ability.

Although The Fundamental Relationship is circular, it all starts with you. The relationship begins when you decide to use your Unique Ability to create value for others. To do this consciously, you must first understand your Unique Ability. However, many people — for example, most entrepreneurs — make this decision without knowing their Unique Ability. They simply decide that they will create value for others before they expect anything in return. The advantage of having a conscious understanding of your Unique Ability is that you get to create value by doing what you love to do. This means your efforts have the force of your passion and your natural talents behind them. This passion and talent are what carry entrepreneurs, artists, and other innovators who are up against unfavorable odds through tough times on the road to success.

People often get stuck doing activities they are good at but have no passion for. In many situations, it takes courage to decide that you're going to commit to focusing more on your Unique Ability. It can require changing habits, activities, jobs, attitudes, relationships, and many other circumstances.

However, in return for facing these challenges, you can have a life that is constantly fulfilling and that always offers greater opportunities for growth, accomplishment, and contribution. You will not be one of the people who says, "Is this all there is?"

> *Marilyn describes her Unique Ability as "seeking and creating high-trust, alternative environments to discover the heart of the matter, so people can shift their perceptions and align with the essence of who they are and what they want to do." You may need to read that a few times because it's quite dense with content, which is not unusual for a Unique Ability Statement. However, it does accurately reflect what Marilyn does in all situations where she creates value with her Unique Ability. Marilyn has been committed to the principles embodied in this statement for years, even though she'd never captured them in this way before.*

Creating value.

Your Unique Ability hits the world when you use it to create value for others. Let's look more closely now at how this happens. There are several aspects to this top portion of the diagram where your Unique Ability

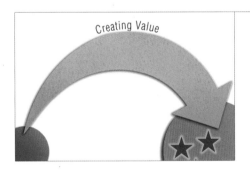

connects with the world. You use your Unique Ability to create value for a specific audience or audiences. The vehicle for this value creation is a particular skill set, process, habit, or activity which is really just a distribution channel that allows you to express your Unique Ability. When you express your Unique Ability through a distribution channel for a particular audience, you create a

The Value Creator™

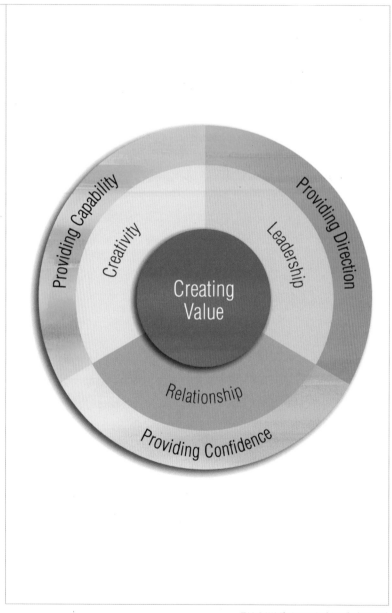

unique experience for that audience that no one else can duplicate. Let's examine each of these components in more detail so you can see how to make them work for you.

What is value creation?

The term "value creation" has been used here a number of times, and it's important to be clear what is meant by these words, which are so often used and so seldom defined. In Strategic Coach® terms, everyone creates value for others through three types of activities: Leadership, providing direction; Relationship, providing confidence; and Creativity, providing capability. Value is only created if the recipient perceives that they have been provided one or a combination of these three things.

- **Leadership — providing direction.**
  Direction can be provided by eliminating someone's "dangers," by helping them to maximize their opportunities, and by creating a plan or a path for them to progress.

- **Relationship — providing confidence.**
  Confidence can be provided by reducing uncertainty. This can be done by ensuring a more predictable future or a less bumpy road, or by creating stability through a sense of safety, reliability, or groundedness in some area that is important to the other person.

- **Creativity — providing capability.**
  Capability is what most people identify with value creation. It includes providing new resources, skills, opportunities, products, services, knowledge, and perspectives — basically anything that helps others accomplish their goals and better their lives in some desirable way.

In our experience, applied Unique Ability always creates value in one or a combination of these ways. For example, a singer-songwriter who plays for his or her audience may create value by entertaining them. This is providing the capability for the listeners to have a good time. They may also provide direction through the content of their songs and how they're delivered. Many a person has experienced new insight through exposure to music or other forms of art. If the person has seen this performer before and knows they put on a good show, the singer is also providing confidence. Past shows have been good, so the audience has confidence that future shows will deliver a similar experience. One of the rewards that a singer gets from creating value in these ways is a following, a group of fans who will pay to see shows and buy records, supporting the continued development of that artist's Unique Ability.

Marilyn was always committed to creating value in whatever situation she was in. Her credo from early on was, "What's needed here? How can I be useful?" Her first career as a nurse gave her the opportunity to listen to and help a wide variety of people, which she loved. What she didn't like were the systems and structures, which she saw as autocratic and hierarchical. Nurses were not often listened to. This was not the ideal environment for her Unique Ability, though she did get to use her listening skills, which she'd had since childhood, with a wider variety of people than she'd ever been exposed to. The main reward she received from nursing was the satisfaction of helping people. Other rewards included appreciation from her co-workers, the satisfaction of being part of a strong team, and the new challenges and growth opportunities of working in different settings, including the high-stakes environment of the operating room where teamwork was paramount.

Your target audiences.

The Fundamental Relationship starts when you decide to use your Unique Ability to benefit others. You do this by creating relationships with specific people or groups of people (target markets or audiences) who value what you can create using your Unique Ability. You've already been doing this subconsciously up to this point in your life. The people you sent your Unique Ability Question to are examples of people who appreciate your Unique Ability. Now that you better understand your Unique Ability and what others value about it, you can consciously go about building relationships with people and groups who will benefit even more from it.

Creating more value is one way to increase the impact of your Unique Ability on the world and the size and number of rewards you receive. Keeping in mind that value is in the eye of the beholder, you can either create more value for a current audience or find a bigger or more appreciative audience. To be very successful, you need not have a big audience. You only need an audience that is willing and able to deliver large rewards in return for the value you create. As Dan Sullivan likes to say, "How much ocean do you really need to swim in? Only the six square yards around you." There are several advantages to serving a small audience. You can build stronger relationships and understand more intimately what each person's real needs are and how to serve them. If it's a business situation, a smaller number of clients and customers may mean less overhead and administration as well as a more personal approach.

The best audiences to build relationships with are those individuals or organizations that both appreciate and nurture your Unique Ability. We all want relationships that create value for ourselves and for others, but common sense and experience tell us that these types of relationships don't happen with everyone. The world is too big. It has too many people, and what people consider to be of value is too diverse for any one individual to cater to everyone. Choosing the best "target markets" for your Unique Ability is a way to speed up its development and increase the size of the rewards you can reap as a result. One of the exercises we have our clients do involves identifying who their ideal client is. The purpose is to get a sense of what their best relationship looks like so they can attempt to "clone" it. For example, Jim M. works with high-net-worth families to clarify their priorities and fulfill their goals. His Unique Ability is "recognizing the opportunity, intuitively understanding the dynamics, imparting a larger vision, outlining a simple path, and bringing the resources together to fulfill the dream." Jim has identified his ideal client as someone having the following ten characteristics:

1. Business owner (or former owner).
2. Estate of $10 million plus.
3. Loves his or her children and their well-being is a key priority.
4. Doesn't want to pay more in tax than necessary.
5. A generous person.
6. Open to new ideas.
7. Wants to bring order out of chaos.
8. Trusting.
9. Minimum age in mid-fifties.
10. Independent thinker.

Marilyn has grown her Unique Ability through working with many different audiences. After leaving nursing to have her first child, she became a stay-at-home mother for seven years. During this time, her main audience was her husband and her two daughters. Her Unique Ability was focused on finding alternatives to autocratic models of parenting. This involved getting to know her children, listening to them and what they wanted, and allowing them to express themselves. During this time, she discovered a "trust community" that introduced her to ways of being and thinking that were much more akin to how she felt inside than most of the world she'd been exposed to. From being in this community, she developed the notion that the most useful thing she could teach her children was to trust themselves and their own intuition. This was a radical alternative to the protective approach that teaches children to trust others' perceptions rather than their own. Marilyn has successfully used her Unique Ability not only with her two children, but with the inner city's most disturbed and delinquent adolescents; the employees and management of a large supermarket chain and a large bakery organization; clients of her own personal growth business; and with coaches, team members, and entrepreneurial clients of The Strategic Coach. Each of these audiences has been increasingly receptive to what Marilyn has to offer, and for each of these audiences in succession she has been able to create more value. Why such varied audiences, you may ask? Each of these opportunities came to Marilyn through the recommendation of someone she had known or worked with, who had seen her Unique Ability in action and realized that it might be a fit for a different kind of situation. Because Marilyn's Unique Ability is so much about transforming people through real human connection, it was completely transferable to any situation where people were at the heart of the matter.

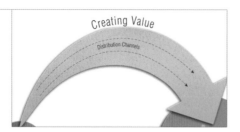

Distribution channels — tying it together.

A distribution channel is a skill, activity, habit, or process that you use to deliver your Unique Ability to an audience in a way that creates value. Basically, distribution channels are vehicles for your talent and passion. When your Unique Ability is expressed through a distribution channel, the result is a unique experience for a particular audience. No one else can duplicate what your Unique Ability and your skills together combine to create. Positive reinforcement from the right audiences further fuels the desire to add to your repertoire of skills, capabilities, and resources in this area. Because they appreciate it, you do more, and you strive to do it even better.

You may find that you use many different distribution channels to create value for different audiences in different situations. People may think you have many unrelated skill sets, but, really, these talents are all tied together by one Unique Ability. For instance, someone who is passionate about and talented at "pulling together something extraordinary and unexpected from diverse elements in the moment" may be very good at cooking without using recipes, at transforming customer service messes, at improvisational performance, and at pulling together the scattered thoughts of groups of people and putting them into words that everyone can agree on. These may seem like unrelated activities, but they are all distribution channels that tap into the same Unique Ability. Look back at the Unique Ability activities you identified in your Unique Ability Snapshot to see what some of your current distribution

Distribution channels
are vehicles for your
talent and passion.

channels are. Here are some examples of other people's Unique Abilities and some of the varied distribution channels they use to create unique experiences for others: Barb D.'s Unique Ability is "recognizing and thoughtfully arranging the details to achieve honest connections with people to inspire growth." Her distribution channels include activities such as training, coordinating events, rearranging the kitchen supplies while camping, and documenting and sharing teams' successful processes. Russell's Unique Ability involves "nurturing human progress." He creates value with it through client meetings, family conversations, innovating ideas for home improvement projects, coaching, and developing meaningful personal relationships.

Your Unique Ability is innate, but the distribution channels you use to turn it into something real in the world still require focus and practice to develop. Often people begin to develop them naturally from a young age, driven by the positive feedback they receive. Because they derive such passion and energy from the results of their efforts, people tend to have more interest in developing skill sets and gaining experience in areas that are outlets for their Unique Ability than in those that aren't. Still, these efforts can be thwarted by feelings of guilt about doing only what you love, by a sense that well-roundedness is better than specialization, and by other kinds of negative associations and conditioning. For instance, some people are conditioned to believe that a particular kind of skill or mode of expression is "inappropriate," or "impractical" based on someone else's idea of who they are or what they should be doing with their life. Nonetheless, most people manage to create several distribution channels without even really being conscious of what their Unique Ability is.

Once you do know what it is, you can be more strategic about choosing and focusing on the best distribution channels to achieve your goals.

You probably have many more potential distribution channels than you're currently using. New channels can be useful to create new career opportunities, satisfying hobbies, extra pursuits outside your career, or a more balanced life. For example, if you found, when you did your Activity Snapshot that most of your Unique Ability activities were work-related, you might want to look for some distribution channels that you can use in other parts of your life. These would include skill sets and activities that allow you to contribute your Unique Ability in different circumstances with different audiences, such as family and friends. Even better might be ways to use your Unique Ability in concert with theirs to create something together.

Keep in mind that, just as others see your Unique Ability more clearly than you do, others may see new distribution channels for your Unique Ability more easily than you do. Pay attention when people bring you new opportunities to use your Unique Ability in different arenas.

Each audience Marilyn has served has given her the opportunity to develop different skills and processes through which she channels her Unique Ability. Some of the distribution channels she has developed and used at different times include nursing, coaching, consulting, writing, creating workshops, parenting, and one-on-one counselling. Her work with the bakery and supermarket chains allowed her to develop highly effective and innovative processes for human resources development that drew on her unique perspective. The trust she fostered at all levels in these organizations and her alternative ways of seeing situations took her beyond traditional HR functions to mediating labor relations issues and resolving productivity issues. At each career and life change opportunity, Marilyn was aware at some level that the right decision lay in following her passion and allowing her Unique Ability a chance to grow and develop in a new arena. She was fortunate enough to be this self-aware. Her ability to shift her own perceptions to align them with the essence of who she was contributed to her willingness to follow a path that many others would find too risky to contemplate.

As a housewife in a small town, she remembers seeing other wives a few years her senior at various social functions and thinking to herself, "That's me in ten years. I don't want to go down that path." Though comfortable, this life was not a fit for Marilyn. She knew there had to be more. Her passions took her out into the community where she saw what was needed and made it happen. A nursery school and a live theater company sprang up where there had been none.

At a workshop for people who were active in their communities, her first experience with adult education, she got a powerful new sense of the value of her own thinking. "I felt like my brain had been let out of jail." Energized by her new-found discoveries, she visited other housewives, taking them Carl Rogers' book, Freedom to Learn, *hoping to find some kindred spirits that would share her excitement. This led to a burning interest in further education. There were tools, ideas, philosophies, and concepts that could enrich her ability to do what she was passionate about.*

With the support of her husband, she came to the city to study adult education, human relations, and group dynamics. This education gave her the skills and credibility to begin to get paid for using her natural talents in a more focused way. Each successive opportunity allowed her to enhance her skills and further her own understanding of what she has now identified as her Unique Ability. This was a critical factor in her decision to accept these new challenges. When offered an opportunity to become a head trainer for a very successful large corporation, she turned it down and instead started her own business, a much riskier move, because she knew the job would not be a place where she could express her deepest interests and commitments. What took Marilyn into each of these new areas where she was able to successfully develop a new distribution channel was the recommendation of someone who had seen her Unique Ability in action somewhere else. She would never have thought to move from working with youth to working in human resources in the food industry, but others saw the potential for a fit. When she looked further into what was needed, it turned out to be a good opportunity. By understanding where her talents and passion lay, Marilyn profited from being open to opportunities that came from directions she would never have pursued on her own. Though her career path may look like it meanders, there is actually a very clear progression when understood from the perspective of developing her Unique Ability through a series of successively more fruitful distribution channels to different audiences.

What distribution channels do you use to create value with your Unique Ability? Do you use different channels with particular audiences, for instance at home or with your friends, versus at work or at school? Label a new page in your notebook "My Distribution Channels" and list all the activities where you deliver your Unique Ability to an audience in a way that creates value. Use your Activity Snapshot as a starting point, then add in activities from all areas of your life.

> *When you follow your bliss … doors will open where you would not have thought there would be doors, and where there wouldn't be a door for anyone else.*
>
> **Joseph Campbell**

Rewards

The rewards — what you get back.

When a distribution channel connects particularly well with an appreciative audience, you get rewards that encourage you to keep developing it. For entrepreneurs whose distribution channels are embodied in a business, these include profits, revenues, referrals, reputation, and opportunities, among other things. For an individual, money may come to mind first, but within The Fundamental Relationship, the benefits are much more diverse.

Rewards come in many forms. Because you've been creating value for others using your Unique Ability for most of your life without knowing it, you've probably already experienced some of these kinds of rewards. An employer or a customer may give you money or enhance your reputation, whereas family or friends may reward you with loyalty, love, and a sense of security. Making a Unique Ability contribution also has its own benefits, such as the sense of satisfaction that comes with making a difference and being given the opportunity to get better and better at something you love to do. All of these rewards can add up to a great quality of life. Earning them by doing what you're passionate about also makes it a meaningful life.

Getting the world to fund your Unique Ability.

The big, overarching reward that The Fundamental Relationship delivers is that the more you use your Unique Ability to create value for the right audiences, the more the world supports and funds its ongoing development. The bottom line is that you'll get to put more time, energy, and resources into getting better at what you love to do. In Marilyn's example, this happened through people recognizing her unique talents and offering her opportunities to apply them in different ways. Each of these successive opportunities provided a new environment in which to grow new capabilities and hone her understanding of how to create value doing just what she was passionate about. This reward was much more important to Marilyn than money or material security. Each new role allowed for a new evolution of Marilyn's Unique Ability. She has developed a genius for being able to broach difficult personal issues with people head on and help them create effective breakthroughs, a process which brings her tremendous satisfaction. In her current position, she has more leverage to create value for a greater number of people than ever before with less effort. This gives her energy and excitement about future possibilities and the impact she can have. The organization she is working with has goals, a purpose, and a Unique Ability of its own that are aligned with what Marilyn needs to develop her Unique Ability to an exponentially higher level. Not only is she able to use her own distribution channels — the various skills and processes she has learned and developed over the years — she is also able to tap into the organization's distribution channels of coaching and product development to get more of her wisdom out to a greater number of appreciative people. And for the value she is able to create within these structures, she is being paid better than ever before, with the added bonus of being able to work closely with both of her daughters.

The upper reaches.

Some people are afraid of heights. Unlimited possibility can be daunting, but a large part of what frightens people is the unknown. When people have the opportunity to focus on their Unique Ability and build their Fundamental Relationship over a period of many years, truly amazing things can happen. We offer the following examples to inspire and prepare you. As long as you stay focused on your Unique Ability and don't get distracted, you'll have the opportunity to realize three extraordinary possibilities: first, the possibility of being seen as a genius; second, Dan's "greatest secret" from the quote that began this chapter — "do what you love, make a great contribution, and get extraordinarily well-paid for it"; and third, creating a life with a sense of endless possibility.

1. A different kind of genius.

Many people think genius is a matter of having a high I.Q. or that it's something a very select few are born with. However, the kind of genius that's responsible for most practical achievements in the world actually comes from focusing on an area of Unique Ability over a long period of time. Muhammad Ali, who scored 78 on an I.Q. test as a young man, was considered a genius as a boxer. There are many possible areas of genius that have little or nothing to do with pure cognitive intelligence and everything to do with Unique Ability. For instance, great artists, athletes, chefs, and performers are often referred to as geniuses.

> *Neither a lofty degree of intelligence nor imagination nor both together go into the making of genius. Love, love, love, that is the soul of genius.*
>
> **Wolfgang Amadeus Mozart**

Perhaps you've heard the expression, "an overnight success ten years in the making." Unique Ability genius is like that: Geniuses have a way of making things look so natural and easy, but arriving at that point takes a lot of work. In our experience, to achieve genius-level performance takes roughly 10,000 hours, or ten years, of concerted focus, on an area of Unique Ability. Cyclist Lance Armstrong, who overcame cancer and went on to win the Tour de France numerous times once said, "Everybody wants to know what I'm on. What am I on? I'm on my bike busting my ass six hours a day. What are you on?"

Unique Ability geniuses perform at a level that astonishes others. Their innate understanding of the area in which their genius lies is truly exceptional. They're able to accomplish spectacular results with an ease that impresses even the talented and leaves laypeople completely amazed. They display evident mastery and are generally quite humble about it, because it comes so easily and, though they so far surpass others' abilities, they still see how much more progress there is to make, and this is their focus.

Can you imagine what your life would be like if you could get to the essence of who you are and what you're about, then focus on doing as much of that as possible over the next ten years — applying yourself to more and more opportunities and activities and working with audiences who use, appreciate, enhance, reward, and tell others about your amazing Unique Ability? What could you accomplish? How would you feel? Would that be a worthwhile goal for yourself?

2. The greatest secret.

The idea of doing what you love, making an enormous contribution to the world, and getting paid extremely well for it is pretty appealing to most people. But many believe it can't be done. Our clients prove every day that it can, with an entrepreneurial mindset, a strong commitment to building structures that support and leverage your Unique Ability, and the knowledge, attitudes, skills, and habits needed to build these structures, it's definitely possible. Not surprisingly, the ways in which our clients have realized this third secret are completely unique: a janitorial company that enables its employees to buy their own homes and learn English through special programs, while providing better service at a lower price than any of its competitors; a financial advisor who is responsible for the biggest shipment of medical supplies in history to Belarus; a former lawyer and financial advisor who has reduced the costly and adversarial process of getting a divorce to a series of six amicable steps, and who is now selling this know-how to others at higher margins than traditional legal or financial services have ever returned.

3. How far can I go?

As your Unique Ability develops through the evolutionary cycle of The Fundamental Relationship and delivers all the rewards you ever thought you wanted and more, you may achieve a sense of mastery, and a feeling of ease. This is not the same as the complacency that comes from coasting along at something that no longer challenges you. You may want to change your role, but you'll probably never want to retire from developing and using your Unique Ability — it's too compelling. It's much more likely that you'll always be driven to go even further, if for no other reason than that you can. When he was six years old, standing in a field in winter watching a plane fly overhead, Dan Sullivan was struck by the question, "I wonder, how far can I go?" The Fundamental Relationship is the structure that ensures that there are no limits to creating the life you want.

> It offers the freedom to do what you love, on your own terms, and to have the world fund your personal growth in return for the value you create.

Freedom to own your future.

Understanding your Fundamental Relationship with the world leads to freedom because it puts you in charge of the elements that determine your own happiness and the direction and size of your future. It offers the freedom to do what you love on your own terms and to have the world fund your personal growth in return for the value you create. It also frees you up from having to devote your life to energy-draining activities and situations. It alleviates the confusion and frustration that come from not knowing how to make the greatest contribution or how to integrate what's meaningful and energizing to you into your daily activities. There are many ways and places to use our Unique Abilities in the world. Entrepreneurs have found their outlet in the marketplace, creating products and services for specific target groups. Other people will find new and different ways to use their Unique Abilities and to create environments in which to grow them.

The world does not owe you the opportunity to do only what you love.

What makes it all work.

Having done the exercises in Chapter 2, you can probably see that you're already in a Fundamental Relationship with the world, even though you've never thought about it in these terms before. To take charge of this relationship, you need to make a commitment to three basic attitudes and principles:

1. The No-Entitlement Attitude™.

The Fundamental Relationship, and all it promises, begins with this essential attitude: Rewards only flow reliably to those who first create value for others. Entitlement attitudes of any kind are poisonous to value creation. Fortunately, we can cleanse them from our belief systems if we become aware of their presence. It's very important not to fall into the trap of using Unique Ability as an excuse. The world does not owe you the opportunity to do only what you love. You get to do it because it creates value for others. You've discovered the right audience and are making that value creation happen. *You* need to take charge of creating the conditions where you can use your Unique Ability. You are the only one you can rely on to be committed to that goal.

This is the true joy in life, the being used for a purpose recognized by yourself as a mighty one; the being thoroughly worn out before you are thrown on the scrap heap; the being a force of nature instead of a feverish selfish little clod of ailments and grievances complaining that the world will not devote itself to making you happy.

George Bernard Shaw

2. Leave behind rugged individualism.

Though The Fundamental Relationship begins with you making a decision to create value, it's not just about you. In fact, without others, you won't get very far. In order to focus on your Unique Ability most productively, you'll need to partner with others who have complementary Unique Abilities. Thinking you need to do this all yourself or that you'll somehow be better off going it alone will only lead to frustration and limited possibilities. This is a time to embrace the idea of building a Unique Ability Team, which we'll discuss more in the next chapter. Fortunately, the more you put your Unique Ability out into the world to create value, the more the right people will be drawn to you.

3. Face and overcome fear and guilt.

It's important to be honest with yourself about how you feel about embarking on the path of Unique Ability. Though you may be very excited about the possibilities, and you may have a deep sense that you need to move in this direction, it's common to have some apprehensions. Fear and guilt are likely at the root of these. There are many fears that people experience around the notion of Unique Ability and The Fundamental Relationship. Most of them arise out of habits, beliefs, and thinking patterns which have been instilled in us over the years by numerous conscious and subconscious influences. For instance, we feel guilty about doing only what we love because somewhere along the line, we were conditioned to believe that real rewards should only come as a result of "hard work." Identifying your own feelings of fear and guilt so you can examine and overcome them is critical to taking charge of your Fundamental Relationship. As we'll see in the next chapter, you need to look head-on at your obstacles, including fear and guilt, in order to overcome them. Once you consciously examine them, their power to get in your way is greatly diminished.

The Unique Ability Development Plan™.
The surest way to create a situation where you're able to develop your Unique Ability and have other people fund it is to look at your current Fundamental Relationship and come up with strategic ways to strengthen it. Take a page in your notebook, label it "My Unique Ability Development Plan," and explore the following questions:

- How do I use my Unique Ability to create value?
- Who does it create value for now?
- How can I reach more people, increase the value I create for my current audience(s), or both?
- What distribution channels have I developed to express my Unique Ability?
- How can they be strengthened?
- Are there other ways I can create value with my Unique Ability, perhaps for other audiences?
- What rewards do I currently receive?
- What rewards would I like to reap in the future to support the ongoing development of my Unique Ability as well as my quality of life goals?
- What do I need to grow my Unique Ability to the next level?
- How does this fit with the kind of life I'd like to lead?

These are big questions, but don't let the magnitude of them deter you. It's important to remember that this is a lifelong process, and that you're in control of the rate of your own progress. You probably won't have all the answers right now, and that's okay. Even if you did, things would change and evolve in unpredictable ways. That's the way life works. Here's a story that illustrates what we mean:

All my life I've done creative things. My childhood best friend, Karl, was in a wheelchair, so when other kids were outside playing baseball, we were busy inside drawing cartoons. It wasn't a compromise: There was nothing I'd rather have been doing.

When one of my high school teachers told me about a professional cartooning opportunity, I leapt at it. But coming up with material for "Canadian Coin News" and "Canadian Stamp News" was as tough as you might imagine: The only funny thing about the hobbies of numismatics and philately is their names.

By the time I went to university, I'd developed a fascination with acting. My parents, ever supportive (if sometimes bewildered), figured if I could pass the audition, I should do it. Five years later, I had the Actor's Equity card to prove I was a pro. Every weeknight and twice on Saturdays, I went to the theater where I was the lead in a summer stock show. Except for one hitch: I didn't want to do it anymore. Sure, I hated the humiliating rounds of commercial auditions, but here I was with a plum theater gig. What was up? Stretching my emotions so I could honestly cry each night, becoming these other people (always at their most dramatic, conflicted point in life), suddenly didn't feel like something a sane person should do. No wonder movie stars have such messy lives.

So I retired. But this time I didn't have a back-up plan. I worked on a construction job, I worked in a family-run shop, I worked as a waiter — all of which felt like work and had no meaning for me. When my friend Mark pitched the idea of travelling across the country, I knew it was the right thing to do. We weren't trying to find ourselves — we knew who we were, we just wanted to find out what those people were supposed to do.

When we reached the West Coast, I drew endless cartoon postcards to send home. Within a month, my buddy and I headed home, where the postcards bloomed into a handmade greeting card business. (Ironically, I've made my living doing things that got me into trouble at school.) To facilitate production, I bought a computer. Before long, I was working full-time as a computer graphics artist, which got the attention of The Strategic Coach, who hired me for their multimedia team.

In our spare time, my best friend and I wrote, produced, and acted in a show about our travels. Writing was it, the thing. I loved it more than anything I'd ever done. Even in theater school, one of my professors told me he thought I was a good actor, but I'd probably turn into a writer. I didn't listen. But as I look back, I see that I've been writing ever since Mrs. Petryshyn asked us to invent an alternate ending to The Metamorphosis. *Rewriting Kafka now seems like a strange task for a ten-year-old, but I remember loving it and not wanting to stop. Through my teens and twenties, I filled a bookshelf with journals. In my spare time while working at The Coach, I finished and self-published my first novel, and wrote my second book.*

One afternoon, Catherine Nomura asked if I'd be interested in writing for the company. I did a bit of a forehead-slap: Of course!

I was good at multimedia, but the rest of the team was better, and I didn't mind. But writing? Nobody needs to challenge me there, because I've got that built in. People often say, "Oh, you must be so disciplined. I'd love to write a book." But I ask them if they like writing, and they don't. See, I love it. No discipline here, I'm just doing what I want to, what I have to.

When my friends grumble about their jobs, I stifle a grin: I love my life.

So for the past year, I've been a professional writer. I still love the sound of that. I finish my work for the company, and on the weekend I write chapters for my novel. When my friends grumble about their jobs, I stifle a grin: I love my life. Paradoxically, the art that waited for me until I could sit still is also the one that gives me the most freedom to move: I now live in Scotland, which I'd dreamt of for years.

Working through the process in this book, I finally pinned down my Unique Ability: "Describing real and imaginary details so they come to life and people experience a moment of wonder." Now I see that everything else led me to this, trained me for it, in a way I could never have consciously devised. Whether it's the guiding hand of fate or my own persistence, the payoff is just as great. But now that I know why I've been doing all this and what it's in service of, life has become a lot clearer. I'll always have this statement, like a pole-star to guide me.

Hamish M.

You're going to put in the
time anyway, so why not
make the effort to make your
life as fulfilling as possible.

In focusing on building and strengthening your Fundamental Relationship, you're taking charge of creating your own future. No one can do this but you, and there's no roadmap for your experience. It will be challenging, unpredictable, and infinitely rewarding. It will also be a life lived with purpose, direction, and meaning. You're going to put in the time anyway, so why not make the effort to make your life as fulfilling as possible. There are some actions and strategies that can make this path clearer and increase your confidence as you find your way. In the next section, we'll offer suggestions on how to develop your own personal strategy as well as some structures to guide and protect you in your exploration now and into the future.

4.

Creating The Life
You Want

Unique Ability

Creating The Life You Want

Chapter 4:
Creating The Life You Want

*O*ur deepest fear is not that we are inadequate. Our deepest fear is that we are powerful beyond measure. It is our light, not our darkness that most frightens us. We ask ourselves, 'Who am I to be brilliant, gorgeous, talented and fabulous?' Actually, who are you not to be? You are a child of God. Your playing small doesn't serve the world. There's nothing enlightened about shrinking so that other people won't feel insecure around you. We are born to make manifest the glory of God that is within us. It's not just in some of us, it's in everyone. And as we let our own light shine, we unconsciously give other people permission to do the same. As we are liberated from our own fear, our presence automatically liberates others.*"*

Marianne Williamson, in *A Return to Love*
(quoted by Nelson Mandela in his 1994 inaugural speech)

A conscious plan.

As you've seen from the previous chapters, the rewards of living a life built around your Unique Ability are tremendous. Some people, like Marilyn and Hamish, whose stories appeared in the previous chapter, unknowingly shaped their lives around their unique talents and passions long before they were aware of the concept of Unique Ability. They are among the relative few who were somehow instinctively able to see that this was the only way to go. Everyone has the instincts to do what they love and follow their passion.

Unfortunately, many of us override them because of things we're taught or conditioned to believe or because of circumstances that arise in our lives. When we suppress these instincts, we set ourselves up for pain which can become the root of a host of other problems including anger, denial, self-destructive behaviors, arrogance, and apathy. This is why understanding the concept of Unique Ability, knowing yours, and seeing how it can impact your life and the rest of the world through The Fundamental Relationship is so useful. Once you understand Unique Ability, you can give yourself permission to follow your passion and find ways to use your unique talents to create the future you want. You can also become conscious of what's getting in your way as you try to make progress along this path.

The reason the basic ideas behind Unique Ability and The Fundamental Relationship remain a secret to many is that there are numerous common obstacles to seeing and living life this way. Conditioning, complexity, guilt, attachment, and fear are just a few of the things that can keep you from focusing on your Unique Ability. Even if you're committed to discovering your Unique Ability and strengthening your Fundamental Relationship, you may need help to recognize and overcome certain challenges. In this chapter, we'll explore a wide variety of obstacles and how to deal with them. Some of these obstacles are internal, for instance, thoughts, beliefs, habits, and emotions that get in your way. Others are external, such as forces out in the world, or in your environment at home, work, or school.

Obstacles are the raw material for progress.

The particular set of obstacles you face will be completely unique to you based on your circumstances, history, upbringing, beliefs, and goals. Don't avoid them or allow yourself to become discouraged. They're actually very useful. Your obstacles are some of the most important raw material you'll need to shape your life around your Unique Ability. By coming up with a strategy to overcome each obstacle, you'll create a step-by-step path to get to the next level. Once there, along with all the rewards, you'll see new obstacles — the challenges that come with a higher level of success — and these will help you plan to achieve even greater progress. Recognizing obstacles as they come up and dealing with them head-on will keep you on track towards the future you want. The most important ingredients in all of this are a commitment to your Unique Ability and confidence in your own creativity. With these two things, you will always find your own strategies for success and happiness.

Reflecting on your current situation.

The first thing to do is reflect honestly on your current situation. Two important results will come out of this reflection: You'll come face to face with your current obstacles, and you'll create a benchmark from which to measure your progress. It's particularly useful to pay attention to your feelings here, and not just rely on your thoughts. There's a good chance that some of your biggest obstacles are things you haven't figured out yet, or that you may be rationalizing in some way to protect yourself. Obstacles may also arise from the set of other people's unquestioned thoughts, judgements, and ideals that form a part of each of our mental landscapes. Your feelings are a more reliable, if sometimes less accessible, guide. Don't worry if they're mixed. Many people feel both excitement and apprehension when thinking about Unique Ability and its implications. You may feel inspired, validated, trapped, confused, excited, or fearful. More likely, you're experiencing some combination of these emotions. If you aren't sure how you feel, you may want to refer back to the work you did on your Unique Ability Development Plan from the last chapter. What feelings came up when you thought through and answered those questions? Were there any questions that were difficult or uncomfortable to answer?

Sometimes it's easier to recognize what you're feeling when you see or hear an example. In this section, we'll describe some common situations people find themselves in when they first begin to understand the concept of Unique Ability and how it relates to their lives.

Feeling validated.

You might find that Unique Ability changes the way you view your current circumstances, and that there are more opportunities around you than you ever noticed before. Some people find that they can go about the same activities, but in a new way that makes better use of their Unique Ability. Or sometimes they begin to appreciate themselves and their contributions more, just because they see that not everyone can do what they do. They begin to see more clearly what others value about them and are motivated to do more of that. Validation is a feeling that many people experience after identifying their Unique Ability and particularly after having it confirmed by others. For some people, this is enough. They don't feel compelled to go to the next stage and change their actions dramatically. However, when new circumstances and opportunities arise, they factor their Unique Ability into their decision-making processes which will effectively change the course of their lives.

Feeling inspired.

Some people discover what their Unique Ability is and are completely inspired to transform their lives around it. It becomes a beacon that guides them to make dramatic changes that they would never have contemplated before. When your Unique Ability Statement is "bang-on," you may feel a sudden sense of clarity and understanding about your past. All your experiences suddenly make sense in a new way, and you realize that your Unique Ability has led you to where you are today. Many people experience a dramatic boost in confidence when this happens. They realize that they've actually been on track for a long time without being conscious of it. Now, with their new awareness, they can see future possibilities much more clearly and begin to strategize to make them happen. However, there may also be so many possibilities that it's overwhelming or confusing. Inspiration is great fuel, but it needs a focus to lead to productivity and happiness. Keeping your focus on your Unique Ability can be challenging and is best done with the help of others. The tools that are covered later in this chapter offer practical ways to get focused and stay on track so you can make the most of this positive energy.

Feeling overwhelmed.

Some people have a difficult time even believing they have a Unique Ability. Surprisingly, this often happens to very successful people whom you would think would be able to see their Unique Ability in action regularly and experience the results it generates. Many successful entrepreneurs, for example, become so bogged down in the complexity of their businesses that they become completely drained of energy and can't feel excited about anything. Until they delegate some tasks, they have no energy to experience the passion that comes with using their Unique Ability. And, being spread so thin, they may almost never get a chance to use it. The best solution for these people is to give themselves a break — real, rejuvenating time completely away from the source of stress — so they can begin to see clearly again. This is a very difficult thing to do when you're overwhelmed, but it's often a smarter strategy. The perspective and new energy gained can mean that you actually accomplish more in less time on your return. Even one full day away from it all can make a significant difference.

Feeling trapped.

There are many kinds of traps that keep people from focusing on their Unique Ability. If you're feeling trapped, it may be by circumstances, such as family responsibilities, that prevent you from making changes in your life that you'd like to make. Or it may be by a relationship with a person, a company, or a job that gives you comfort, security, status or other rewards, but that doesn't allow you to do what you're passionate about. Learning about Unique Ability sometimes allows people to see more clearly just how trapped they really are. It's a lot harder to make do with the status quo once you see that there are greater possibilities available, particularly if you don't yet know how to realize those possibilities. However, until you see your trap, you can't get out of it. Here are a couple of examples. These are basically true stories. Names and certain details have been changed for purposes of confidentiality.

He was providing an excellent quality of life by other people's standards, but it wasn't the unique quality of life he wanted.

Eric was a wealthy man who had made it to the top of his profession at a young age. He had all the material trappings of success — the big house in a prestigious neighborhood, multiple expensive cars, memberships at the best clubs, a palatial summer home with all the toys, a loving wife, and great kids whom he sent to the best private schools. But deep down, Eric was not happy. He held his unhappiness inside for a long time because he actually felt too guilty to share it. How could he, with everything he had, be unhappy? He felt there must be something wrong with him and kept trying to convince himself that things were really fine. Every once in a while, a crazy thought would go through his mind about giving it all up and running off to do something completely different. To combat these thoughts, he would work harder at a job he was not passionate about, seeing less and less of his family, and spending less and less time enjoying the lifestyle he was financing. Once he understood Unique Ability, he knew the source of his unhappiness, and he no longer felt crazy or ungrateful, just trapped. He had an excellent quality of life by other people's standards, but it wasn't the unique quality of life he wanted.

Leila was superb at her job as a sales representative. Her glowing reviews made her a shoe-in for a much higher paying sales position at a new company. That this job came with a much higher salary was important, since her husband had just decided to go back to school, and she had agreed to be the sole breadwinner for him and their two children. Soon it became apparent that what was required in the new company was quite different than what had made her successful in her old role. Her natural strengths and instincts were not a good fit for the needs of a start-up. Leila struggled to meet minimum standards, and was constantly stressed. Everything was difficult and it took her more time and effort than others in similar roles to get the job done. Because of the time she was putting in, she couldn't even think of looking for another job. Besides, her family desperately needed the income, and where was she going to find another position that paid like this? Leila missed the excitement and energy she felt in her old job, but financial concerns and time constraints meant there seemed to be no turning back. Her growing unhappiness spawned feelings of anger, frustration, and resentment that spilled out into her relationships with others outside of work. She had unwittingly given up the opportunity to use her Unique Ability and couldn't see a way back.

Feeling confused.

Confusion is a feeling that many people experience to some degree once they learn more about Unique Ability. The notion of Unique Ability can very quickly change the way you think about a lot of things. Because it's such a different way of looking at yourself and the world, confusion can arise when you try to reconcile Unique Ability and The Fundamental Relationship with your long-held attitudes, assumptions, and beliefs. Also, if you've been committed to a particular course of action and your Unique Ability surprises you, suggesting that perhaps you should be doing something else, it's easy to become confused. Unique Ability, after all, is just a concept, even if you can't get it out of your head once you hear about it. Should you let a concept change your whole life? Do you have a choice?

Because Unique Ability describes a universal truth, it's hard to escape. Once you know about it, it's difficult to forget. Its proof is all around you, playing out in your life and the lives of others in ways you can suddenly see. Once you've grasped the idea of developing the unique talents that you're passionate about or of getting paid to do what you love to do, it's very hard to let go of these possibilities. If you don't know how to get off the path you're on or go about making these seductive visions a reality, life can become very confusing. Confusion may accompany a sense of being trapped, or it may come as a result of having too many options. Here's another typical story:

Nick was in his first year of college, majoring in film studies. Bright and conscientious, he was a good student, especially in the few subjects that he particularly liked, but he wasn't enthusiastic about the whole school experience. He was really only there because his parents insisted that he get a college degree. Nick's father had two doctoral degrees. His parents had saved for his college education since he was born because they believed that this was such an important part of their son's upbringing. A college education was not a choice, it was an expectation.

Nick loved his parents and didn't want to disappoint them, but his real passion lay in what could loosely be called "experience planning." Since he was a young teenager, he had been organizing increasingly successful parties and events for young people. He had become somewhat of a legend and had a following of fans who would come out to anything he put on. Everyone around loved the infectious energy and enthusiasm he radiated when he was trying to make something memorable happen. By the time he graduated from high-school, Nick had developed skills and displayed talent that many professional event planners would envy. His passion for bringing together the creative concept and logistical details to create a unique and unforgettable experience for people had driven him to learn quickly.

However, Nick's parents didn't consider this a real profession. College would prepare him for "something better."

When Nick found out about the concept of Unique Ability, he was fascinated. At first, the idea just sat there in his head and wouldn't go away. What was he passionate about, what was he good at? It seemed clear that it came out in event planning, but not in anything he was doing at school. Soon, his thoughts began to keep him awake at night. Why was he spending four years — all this time, energy, and money — to do something he didn't love? There was nothing in what he was learning that excited him the way planning events did. How could he even broach the subject with his parents? Could he ever be successful in their eyes doing what he had been doing for fun as a teenager? Would people pay him to do it as a full-time job? Where could he learn what he'd need to know to take his skills to the next level? Would he still love it if he did it "for a living?" The questions wouldn't leave him alone. Nick was confused and uncertain about how to take charge of his future.

It's usually much easier to control what goes on inside your own mind than to try to change external circumstances.

A mindset for progress.
Do any of the emotions in these stories resonate with you? Your obstacles may seem easier or more difficult to overcome. Or perhaps they're completely different. Each person whose story we've told faces a number of obstacles, which, when combined, create the feelings described. Some of these are mental, some are circumstantial. Some of them are personal, and some are tied in with other people's hopes, expectations, ideals, and needs. It's usually

much easier to control what goes on inside your own mind than to try to change external circumstances or other people's thoughts and feelings, so this is where we'll start.

Going against gravity.

Throughout our lives, our thinking patterns, beliefs, habits, attitudes, and values are conditioned by many external forces. These forces hold us down mentally, just as naturally and invisibly as the force of gravity holds us down physically. Parents, teachers, mentors, media, advertising, friends, colleagues, peer groups, and numerous other influences pattern our behavior every day without us being completely aware of their influence. As a result of this conditioning, some of the biggest obstacles to focusing on Unique Ability arise out of strong subconscious patterns in our minds that remain unquestioned. When we make them conscious, we're able to see them differently and gradually free ourselves from their influence. Instead of repeating the same behaviors, we can build the "mental muscles" to go against gravity and take a path of our own choosing to new heights. Review the following common obstacles to see how much gravity you're fighting.

Sixteen Common Obstacles.

Most obstacles to focusing on Unique Ability begin in the mind. They fall into the basic categories of fears, limiting beliefs, and misguided thinking. These are all things that can be overcome strategically once you're aware of them.

1. Fear that there is no Unique Ability.

If your attention has been scattered over a wide range of general activities, or if you've spent a lot of time trying to strengthen your weaknesses, your experience of Unique Ability will be limited. You might even think that you don't have one. You may not have looked at your life and activities from a Unique Ability perspective before. It might help to take some time off to see the bigger picture. Another very effective strategy is to enlist the help of someone else who can understand the big picture of what you do. A trusted peer, colleague, friend, or mentor, or even the person you report to may be a good choice. Have them work on The Activity Inventory and Activity Snapshot exercises from Chapter 2 with you. If they know you well, they'll probably have more perspective on where your Unique Ability lies than you do in your state of overwhelm. Let them give you suggestions on how to do fewer of the activities that don't make the most productive use of your abilities and more of those where you can make the greatest impact.

2. Fear that you can't make a living using your Unique Ability.

You may look at your current Unique Ability activities and wonder how you can make a living doing just those things. Or, if you're not using your Unique Ability at all to earn money currently, it may be a

> It usually takes at least three years to make a major shift in the direction of your life.

stretch to think about how you could build a career around it. Getting your Unique Ability Statement as accurate and all-encompassing as possible can broaden the sense of possibility you have for applying your Unique Ability to different kinds of activities and professions. It may take some effort to find the right audience that fully appreciates the value you can provide and to develop the right distribution channel to reach them. Even if you see what you could do that would allow you to create value using your Unique Ability, it may take a different set of skills than you currently have. This is when it's especially important to remember that this is a lifetime process. Give yourself some time to make changes. It usually takes at least three years to make a major shift in the direction of your life. Three years is the amount of time most people need to change their knowledge, attitudes, skills, and habits and bring them into alignment with a new vision. If you create a plan, set clear goals for yourself along the way, and remain committed, real change is possible. We see this with our entrepreneurial clients every day.

Another thing to remember is that your path will be unique. You'll probably be pioneering it yourself. Give yourself credit for this effort and expect a lot of learning from experience along the way. Building a unique path has its own rewards and offers the greatest potential for freedom and happiness. Many people don't realize this because, unless they know a successful entrepreneur or are one themselves, it's not what they've been exposed to.

Some of the most visible examples of people evolving their Unique Ability to a high level and getting paid extremely well for it come from the entertainment industry, including professional sports. Where would Wayne Gretzky have been without hockey, the NHL, and all the feeder systems and structures that produce and provide an income for world-class hockey players? Top entertainers and athletes can benefit from whole industries that are devoted to the development, packaging, distribution, and sales of the products of their Unique Abilities. The rewards that are available through these systems encourage would-be stars to focus on developing their abilities in the ways that fit what the system needs. The dream, the vision, and the path are clear.

Unfortunately, only a very few ever reap the really big rewards in these systems. Most Unique Abilities have no such structures built to connect them with their audiences. Most people have to shape their own dream, find their own path, and form their own vision. There are many benefits to building your own structures. The most obvious is that you get to shape the vision of your own success and the nature of the relationship with your audience and retain a large degree of control over them. Because you're in charge, your chances of success are actually much greater and the degree of your success is limited only by your vision.

3. The Excellence Trap.
If you've done The Activity Inventory exercise in Chapter 2, you already know the difference between excellent and Unique Ability activities: Excellent activities are

those for which you have a superior skill but no passion. Others rely on you to do these things just because you do them so well. Excellent activities are often psychologically difficult to delegate because you know you do a great job and someone else may not do them as well. You may also receive significant praise and financial rewards that compel you to keep doing them. But this can be a trap. Because you have no passion for these activities, you feel unfulfilled at a deep level. Also, the opportunity cost is high because these things stand in the way of your Unique Ability. As long as you're doing them, your time and energy aren't free for concentrating on the things you most love — the areas where you have the potential to make a truly unique contribution to the world. Why settle for excellent when you're capable of unique? Yet many people get trapped focusing on excellent activities all their lives.

You may want to take a look at your excellent activities and see if you feel trapped. Do you feel unable to give them up because you enjoy the praise, the money or the perks, or because you don't want to hand them over to someone who might not do as good a job? Are you talented and successful but bored? If the answer is "yes" to any of these questions, you may need to create a strategy to get out of the trap. If there's a Unique Ability activity that you could be doing instead that would generate even better results, it may be worthwhile to give up the excellent activity. Even if you have to delegate it to someone who's not as good at it, your productivity may go up exponentially and make up the difference. But many people find that they don't really know how to do more of their Unique Ability activities within their current circumstances, whereas there's a big demand for their excellent abilities. Getting clearer on the essence of your Unique Ability by defining your Unique Ability Statement will help you be more creative about how to apply your talents in different ways.

Many people have made successful "leaps of faith" in order to pursue their Unique Ability.

4. Fear of starting over.

If you're very invested in your current situation, for example, you've spent a lot of time, effort, and money on training or moving up a hierarchy, it may be scary to think of leaving it behind. If it's very clear that your Unique Ability cannot be used in your current circumstances, you may have a difficult choice to make. You'll have to weigh the value of a life spent in an unhappy situation against the cost of leaving that situation. Many people have made successful "leaps of faith" in order to pursue their Unique Ability. This is a time to think carefully and be strategic, but also to believe in your own uniqueness and its capacity to create value and open doors you may not be able to see yet. Look for ways that you can use your current situation to fund the shift to a new role. Remember to give yourself time to make the changes. It may take a few years to fully make the shift. Just knowing you're moving toward your goal to use your Unique Ability more, should give you energy and help get you through the transition period. Be sure to track and celebrate your progress, including unforeseen benefits.

Look for ways that you can use your current
situation to fund the shift to a new role.

5. Fear of success.

As the Marianne Williamson quote so eloquently states at the beginning of this chapter, many people are more afraid to face the responsibility of living up to their potential than they are of simply being mediocre all their lives. It definitely takes more commitment to push oneself to be one's best and to seek out one's greatest contribution than to live an unexceptional, and probably unexamined life. Perhaps this is why there are so many who would oppose the person who is determined to stick to the goal of doing only what he or she is unique at. Any struggling artist who has been implored to "get a real job" knows this well. As Mark Twain is reputed to have said, "Keep away from people who try to belittle your ambitions. Small people always do that, but the really great make you feel that you, too, can become great." Our hope is that the exercises and the path offered in this book will help people to overcome any fears they may have and embark joyfully on the path to developing their own greatness, knowing that everyone has this power within them. Those who choose to do so will undoubtedly inspire countless others along the way.

The key to keeping your head on straight once you become successful is simply to view what you're doing as completely normal, for you. The fact that others may be awed by your Unique Ability in action is not that surprising. It's your Unique Ability not theirs, and you've put in the work to make it shine. When Unique Ability gets developed to genius level, it becomes difficult for others to understand how you do what you do. People tend to have two reactions to things they don't understand: fear or reverence. If you're very successful, you may inspire either or both. Neither of these external reactions has anything to do with the reality that you are just pursuing the natural path of developing your Unique Ability — an option that everyone has. As long as you keep your focus on that task and keep drawing energy from the satisfaction that it alone gives you, you'll be able to keep your success in perspective and keep moving ahead.

6. Fear of being too concentrated or being boxed in.

The basis of this belief is that safety lies in being involved in everything, that in being too concentrated you might miss out on important information and events, and that in concentrating on just one area you might somehow choose the wrong one. However, the more you understand your Unique Ability, the more you'll see how it relates to a variety of activities and relationships. Varying the distribution channels through which you use your Unique Ability to create value for different audiences will help speed up its development and offer you different avenues to gain insight into how to apply it better in different areas.

7. Working on your weaknesses.

There's a school of thought, closely related to the idea of being well-rounded, that says you should work on your weaknesses. But here's what you get when you work on your weaknesses: strong weaknesses. What good are they? The fact is that there isn't enough time to get good at everything. Besides that, if you're not good at something by now, there's probably a reason: Maybe you're just not interested. And that's okay!

Is it all right to shirk your responsibilities? Of course not: The consequences would hinder your plans and wreak havoc on your relationships. But instead of wasting time trying to build strong weaknesses, why not try to find someone for whom this is a Unique Ability? It's important not only to identify where you have Unique Ability, but also where you don't, and to allow others to contribute to you in those areas.

> *Except for your unique capability to be you, other people are better at everything else.*
>
> **Dan Sullivan**

8. Unwillingness to give up control.

This comes from the fear that you'll lose control if you don't do everything yourself. In Chapter 3, we talked about leaving behind "rugged individualism." One of the great things about Unique Ability is that it gives you permission not to be great at everything. You are best at your Unique Ability. Others with other Unique Abilities are best at everything else. Do what you're best at and let them do what they're best at, and everyone is better off. You can direct the process by setting a clear goal or providing a vision that everyone can align themselves with. You can be in charge without being in control.

9. Unwillingness to trust others.

This comes in two forms: unwillingness to trust that others can do things as well as you can, and unwillingness to trust that they aren't out to oppose or disrupt your goals. Often, these are simply unfounded negative beliefs or excuses we use to cling to rugged individualism. If you find yourself having these kinds of thoughts, ask yourself, "Is this really true?" and "How would I like things to be different?" Then you can look at the facts of the situation objectively and decide what to do. In the first case, it may be true that someone can't do something as well as you can, but does that mean *you* should be doing it? In the second case, you might want to ask yourself if they really understand your goals. Often what looks like opposition is simply the result of miscommunication or misunderstanding. Building trust with those who can support your Unique Ability is vital. People who operate from arrogance or paranoia eventually thwart their own efforts.

10. Fear of dependency.

Another element of rugged individualism, this fear comes from a belief that you can't be in a position where others are crucial to you. But to expand your capabilities, you have to trust that others won't hold your future hostage and know that their contribution is, in fact, what makes your goals possible.

11. Unwillingness to give up activities.

There are certain things you've done for so long, it's hard to imagine not doing them. Some people get confused, and can't separate their identity from the things they do. Developing your understanding of your Unique Ability gives you permission not to be good at everything and to let go of things you're not passionate about. If you're still having difficulty with giving up activities even after doing the exercises in Chapter 2, you may want to have others help you. Talk to the people you create value for and ask them: "What should I do more of?" and "What should I do less of?" Their answers will give you a different perspective on what they value most about what you do. A supervisor, manager, or mentor who knows you well can also be a useful person to do this with. If you are a manager or team leader, try asking the people on your team for feedback. You may be surprised by their answers. Remember that all your activities are just distribution channels for who you are. Your Unique Ability is more fundamental than any of the ways you use it.

Another thing that sometimes stops us from getting help is that we know we're better at an activity than others. However, it's crucial to look at the end result. Is it better that it get done more slowly than not at all? If you are too busy to get it done, it ultimately makes more sense to partner with someone else. Or perhaps you're unique at one part of the activity, but merely excellent at another. Breaking the activity down and focusing on the part that you're unique at and delegating the excellent part can be a very strategic decision.

Partnering with others is an investment in your Unique Ability.

12. Worry about the cost.

Giving up activities to others might involve taking on new expenses. For instance, if you decide to hire a house cleaner, you'll have to pay that person. After all, they're creating value for you, not just by doing a job that you'd rather not do, but also by freeing up time you can put to better use. Partnering with others is an investment in your Unique Ability. If you do it strategically, the costs should be more than outweighed by the benefits, financially and otherwise.

13. Fear that there'll be nothing left to do.

Some people believe they have to justify their existence by keeping busy. In fact, their identity is tied to doing certain kinds of activities or fulfilling a particular role. If they gave up all those extra activities, what would they do to fill their time? If you're worried your Unique Ability won't give you enough to do, you need to be willing to change your perspective. Unique Ability is a big enough pursuit to provide a lifetime's worth of meaningful activity. And the identity you create around your Unique Ability will be your own and not based on someone else's idea of what you should be doing.

No one can be all things to all people.

14. Fear of being too "out there."

Unique Ability will, by its nature, lead you to do some things differently from the way others do them. Some people are afraid of standing out, worried that they might become the target of others' criticism and opposition. If you're doing what you love and creating value for an appreciative audience, does it matter what others say? No one can be all things to all people. Listen to yourself and to the audience that appreciates you.

15. Guilt about being totally freed up.

Some people have a deeply held belief that they don't deserve to be freed up until everyone is freed up, that others will be resentful and jealous, and that in a world where so many people are unhappy, no one has the right to do only what they love doing. So they prevent themselves from being happier and more successful, which does absolutely nothing to help anyone else to be happier and more successful. Hopefully, if you've read this far, you're at least beginning to see how freeing up your Unique Ability is the best way to increase the contribution you can make to the world.

On a more practical level, many people feel guilty, at least initially, delegating tasks that they don't like, even if they're incompetent at them. Why? Because they think that since they don't like it no one else must like it either. This is simply not true. There are so many different Unique Abilities in the world and so many ways of seeing things that there is a person out there who can bring passion to virtually any task. By holding on to something that you dislike doing, you may be depriving someone who loves to do just that from the opportunity to use their Unique Ability and be rewarded for it.

16. Fear of leaving people behind.

This fear keeps people from making further progress because they believe they're somehow responsible for other people's progress, that their success will make other people unhappy, and that in growing further, they will lose their most important relationships because those people will be unable to relate to them. This fear misses two important points: First, everyone on the planet is responsible for his or her own growth. We can encourage others to grow, but we can't be responsible for their decisions to do so. Second, you're free to take others along for the ride!

What are your obstacles?

A very practical part of your Unique Ability Development Plan that you started in Chapter 3, will be identifying your own obstacles and creating strategies to overcome them. Ironically, a great way to make the obstacles to any goal seem less daunting is to write them all out on one page. Once you see them that way, they become finite and you can deal with them systematically. You can focus on creating a strategy for each obstacle, one at a time, without worrying that countless others are looming. Take a fresh page in your notebook, preferably right after the work you did on your Unique Ability Development Plan, and draw a line down the middle to create two columns. On the left, list as many obstacles to focusing on your Unique Ability as you can think of. Once you've got a complete list, look at each individual obstacle and use the space to the right of it to write down your strategy for overcoming it. Strategies may be as simple as changing the way you think about something. Perhaps you have to catch yourself when you're feeling fear or guilt so you can consciously choose to see the situation differently. Every time you do this, you'll make it easier and more automatic for the next time. Some strategies may involve other people. Some of them may go back to thinking you did for the exercises in Chapter 2. For instance, you may have come up with an improvement idea when doing your Unique Ability Action Plan (after categorizing all your activities) that you can use to overcome an obstacle you've identified here. Feel free to include those strategies and use this as a place to bring together all the relevant thinking you've done so far on how to move ahead.

Strategies to stay on track.

Your Unique Ability Action Plan from Chapter 2, your Unique Ability Development Plan at the end of Chapter 3, and the strategies you've just come up with, should give you a clear idea of how to begin in earnest to build your life effectively around your Unique Ability. As you forge ahead with the first action steps, the path will become even clearer. Every layer of non-Unique Ability activity you shed will give you more perspective and insight into your Unique Ability and how to use it even more productively. New doors will open and you will see opportunity where there was none before. Opportunities, with all the excitement they bring, present their own challenges. Long-term success and happiness require that you keep your focus on developing your Unique Ability and your Fundamental Relationship. Here are two things you can do to stay on track: First, develop a clear understanding of how to determine the best opportunities for the evolution of your Unique Ability. Second, create a strong support network that will bring opportunities to you and help you capitalize on them. In this section, we'll introduce you to some tools and strategies for developing these structures to support your ongoing success.

Finding and creating great opportunities.

Where opportunity is concerned, most people today don't have too little, they have too much. There are so many possibilities that it becomes difficult to sort through them all and decide which opportunities should receive your limited time, energy, and attention. How much an opportunity supports the development of your Unique Ability is a useful gauge to help make these decisions. Now that you know more about your Unique Ability, you can use some specific strategies to help you differentiate the good opportunities from the not so good. You can also begin to identify what your ideal opportunity looks like so you can seek it out, create it for yourself, or identify it with confidence when it presents itself. The first strategy we'll look at will help you create great opportunities that support the development of your Unique Ability and allow you to create maximum value. Your list of "enabling and disenabling factors" is a quick checklist that's personally tailored to your Unique Ability. It will ensure that you capture all the learning from your experiences so you can more quickly determine what kinds of situations are best for your Unique Ability in the future and seek them out.

Learning from experience.

As you take your Unique Ability to the world, you'll be able to proactively create your own opportunities. In fact, you may need to create your own opportunities to develop your Unique Ability the way you want. Fortunately, much of the raw material you'll need to design a great opportunity from the multitude of possibilities that exists comes from something you have in abundance — your own experience. What you need to know to create opportunities that work for you and for others, is what specific conditions support or enable the effective application of your Unique Ability, and what kinds of conditions or circumstances create obstacles, potential traps, or frustrate your attempts to use your Unique Ability productively. The supportive circumstances are "enabling factors," and the things that get in the way are "disenabling factors." It's useful to have a list of each to assess the quality of any opportunity quickly and objectively.

Enabling and disenabling factors.

Take a page in your notebook and label it "Enabling Factors" and label another "Disenabling Factors." Now take a few minutes to consider your Unique Ability Statement and think about past experiences where you felt you were really able to do what it says. What was true that allowed your Unique Ability to be well-received in this situation? What circumstances, audiences, environmental factors, political factors, relationship factors, or anything else allowed your Unique Ability to create value in this situation? You might want to start by brainstorming. What worked in this situation? What didn't work? Of the things that worked, what can you learn from this that translates into a general rule that could apply to other situations as well? For instance, if your Unique Ability was supported by a particular relationship, what features of that relationship made the difference, and what would you look for in future relationships to try to achieve the same result? Write that general rule on your list of enabling factors. You may get several items from one situation. Usually, there are a number of factors at work any time you're able to create a great result using your Unique Ability.

Once you've looked at the things that worked, look at anything that didn't work. What would you look out for in the future to avoid that situation? This can go on your list of disenabling factors. When you've gone through this thinking process with experiences where your Unique Ability was well-used and appreciated, move on to experiences where it was not so effective or where you felt stifled. What kept you from being able to use your Unique Ability to create value? Again, you may want to start by creating a list of what worked and what didn't work in the situation. Be as honest as you can. If there are others who were in this situation with you, try to get their perspectives as well. Looking at what didn't work, what can you do differently to avoid similar experiences in the future? Transfer these lessons to your list of disenabling factors. Once you have a number of items on each list, you may want to divide them into categories, such as audiences, environment, financial, and any others that seem relevant to your Unique Ability and your experiences. The purpose is to create a checklist that will be a guide as you go about shaping your opportunities. Here's an example:

We were introduced to Perry in Chapter 2. Once again, his Unique Ability is "to identify what is missing or needed — and, in the moment, synergistically combine energy and resources — to proactively create a new, better reality." These factors were drawn from real experiences he has had attempting to use his Unique Ability in different situations. The lists will probably continue to grow as he learns from future experiences.

Perry's enabling factors:

Audiences:
- People or organizations that want to realize a greater vision but are unclear about how to articulate the vision or don't know how to implement the change.
- People who are in a position to implement change (not restricted by factors beyond their control).
- People who are open to receiving external assistance to clarify their vision.
- People who are committed to transformation and are likely to see it through.
- People who appreciate an innovative, cutting-edge vision that is well-executed.

Relationships/Teamwork:
- Partnerships with people who have a Unique Ability to manage the follow-through aspects of realizing a vision, who allow me to focus on creating and clarifying the vision and innovating in the moment.
- People in stable positions of authority who are not likely to be replaced before change can be implemented.

- Team members who are excited by a rapidly changing, innovative, energy-charged environment and who can keep up with periods of intense activity under tight deadlines and get the job done.
- People who are committed to honoring the integrity of a relationship with their chosen audience.

Environments:

- Situations where the full potential is not being realized and participants understand this but lack the time, energy, or vision to transform the current reality.
- Situations where people are being forced to settle for something less than ideal because they don't know how to make it better.
- Situations where no one else sees the root of the problem, but where people are happy to experience a better result that I can lead them to.
- Situations where people don't have the external perspective to see how to get to the next level.

Financial factors:

- Budget is available to fund transformation, and people who want transformation control this budget.
- A ready market is available for the product of the transformation and is willing and able to pay for it.
- The transformation costs very little to implement and returns large financial or non-financial rewards, such as publicity, credibility, or networking potential.

Perry's disenabling factors:

Audiences:

- People or organizations that say they to want transform how they do things but really don't. (This is a trap.)

- People or organizations that want change but aren't in a position to implement it due to factors beyond their control. (This is frustrating.)
- People who are unwilling to buy into a bigger vision if it is spearheaded by someone else. (A recipe for resistance. I can't create value for these people.)
- People or organizations that are committed to maintaining the status quo.
- People who are not open to new ways of doing things.

Environments:
- Situations where there's too much internal politics to be able to come to consensus on a vision for transformation.
- Bureaucratic structures that create impediments to transformation because of procedural rules and policies, lack of strong, focused leadership, lack of overall vision, or low priority on creating the best results.

Shaping new opportunities.

When Perry is creating an opportunity for himself, he can look at these factors and try to shape the situation so that as many enabling factors are present as possible. He can also be on the lookout for disenabling factors and take precautions to avoid them, or decide not to pursue the opportunity if they can't be avoided. As he has more experiences of using his Unique Ability, he can add to both lists. A great habit to develop is to debrief at the end of any major project or undertaking about what worked and what didn't work, and see if there is any new learning that adds to or clarifies what your enabling or disenabling factors are. The more clarity you have about these factors, the more quickly you'll be able to realistically predict success or failure and prevent frustration in any new situation. By looking at your enabling factors, you may be able to see more clearly possibilities for new audiences, distribution channels, or ways to create value within your existing circumstances. You can look at each factor and ask yourself, "Where or with whom is this likely to be the case?" For instance, Perry might ask himself, "Where am I likely to find situations where no one else sees the root of the problem, but where people are happy to experience a better result that I can lead them to?" He could probably identify several kinds of situations where this is true. The best of these will also match other enabling factors. For instance, people in some of these situations may also be in a position to fund change and have the authority to make it happen. He can also narrow down the list by ruling out situations where disenabling factors are likely to be present and unavoidable. While this is not an absolute guarantee of success, it certainly increases the chances that any new opportunity will support the development of his Unique Ability and create a great result.

Analyzing existing opportunities.

As you progress along the path of focusing on your Unique Ability, opportunities will also arise that are not of your own creation. People will want you to work with them on projects or ventures because they see a way that your Unique Ability can contribute. You may receive invitations to try new things that you hadn't thought of before, as we saw in Marilyn's story in Chapter 3. Making the right decisions about what to do and what not to do can be challenging, but it's much easier if you use Unique Ability as a guide. Here's a tool that's useful to help you quickly assess opportunities that come to you as well as those you may already be in the process of pursuing.

The Opportunity Filter™.

Too often, it's easy to get involved in situations that, although intriguing at the outset, actually turn out to be a waste of time, energy, money, and creativity. Experiencing the impact of a number, or sometimes even just one of these non-strategic situations, can bring into question your ability to judge how you can best contribute. This can severely impact your confidence and deter you from taking on new, exciting, and potentially profitable ventures.

One of the ways to "filter" opportunities is to evaluate them through the perspective of Unique Ability. There are five important criteria by which to judge a potential opportunity. Ask yourself, "Does it utilize, appreciate, reward, enhance, and refer my Unique Ability?"

The Opportunity Filter™

Utilize.

If a situation utilizes your Unique Ability, it takes full advantage of your talents, passion, and expertise. If you're working with a team, it takes advantage of your team's Unique Abilities too.

Appreciate.

Do the people involved appreciate what you're doing with them? Do they say thank you? Even for those who say they don't need a lot of feedback, working with people who express their appreciation is a lot more satisfying and rewarding than working with people who are stingy with praise and recognition. They most likely won't appreciate the value you're creating, and if you are charging for what you're doing, won't want to pay you full value either.

Reward.
If this is a paying situation, how well are you being compensated for what you're contributing? If you're doing the work for free, are there other rewards, tangible or otherwise, that you're receiving? The best opportunities are the ones that compensate you well, monetarily or otherwise, for the value you're providing. Examples of non-monetary rewards include additional resources, status, opportunity, travel, and "perks."

Enhance.
By being involved in this situation, are you learning and expanding your knowledge and expertise? To fully develop your Unique Ability, it needs to be used and tested in a number of different circumstances. Like a muscle fiber, your Unique Ability needs to be challenged in order to grow. One of the characteristics of Unique Ability is never-ending improvement — you can always see how to get better. The best opportunities are the ones in which you finish knowing more than when you started.

Refer.
Refer simply means that the people you're working with say great things about you to other people. From The Fundamental Relationship, we know that one of the rewards of using your Unique Ability with the right audience is that you get referred into new opportunities in which to exercise your Unique Ability.

One of the ways to use these five criteria is to assign a scoring scale to each of them, for example, -1 for a negative response, to 5 for the best response. Think back to a situation you contributed to that produced an outstanding result, a "best" situation. How did it score? For each of the criteria, you likely answered a 4 or a 5. Then think about a "worst situation," one that did not turn out as you'd anticipated. How did it score? Compare your two answers, and it will give you a frame of reference against which to evaluate future opportunities. Here's what one of our clients had to say about how using her Unique Ability to filter opportunities has affected her decision-making ability and her confidence:

> *It's a lot easier for me to say no. Before I would take business and think, 'Mm, well, it's not really what I want to do, but I'll do it.' Now I can say, 'This is how we do it. You can get on the page with us like this, or we don't do this work.' And I'm completely clear about that.*

Tracy Quinton

Creating a Unique Ability environment.

The best environment in which to stay focused on building a life around your Unique Ability is one filled with people who are doing the same. Unique Ability changes the way people view the world and their relationships with others. This gives environments based on Unique Ability a particular character. There's a basic understanding that each individual has something potentially valuable to contribute, that no one has to be good at everything, that different Unique Abilities can be combined to create superior results, and that people should be encouraged and allowed the opportunity to develop their Unique Abilities as much as possible. This kind of environment is tremendously supportive of growth and self-actualization, as well as being focused on value creation and mutually beneficial relationships. It's each individual's responsibility to take the initiative to find ways to create value using their Unique Ability, but the support and partnership of others is actually what makes the biggest Unique Ability contributions possible. For this reason, the people you choose to surround yourself with can have a major impact on how you are able to develop your Unique Ability. Whether they be team members, family, community, friends, clients and customers, mentors and teachers, or peers, your best support network will be made up of people who value Unique Ability and understand its potential.

In this section, we'll look at how you can create a strong Unique Ability environment in different areas of your life. Fortunately, because Unique Ability is such a naturally appealing idea to most people, this is not a difficult process to begin. In fact, you may find that just by discovering your own Unique Ability and beginning to communicate it, you've already started to attract like-minded people.

The Unique Ability Magnet.

Unique Ability attracts Unique Ability. Your commitment to focusing on your Unique Ability will draw others to you who either want to support your efforts or to be part of what you are creating. The most productive relationships you can build are with others who are also seeking to expand and create greater value with their Unique Abilities and who recognize that a Unique Ability like yours can help make that happen. When people's Unique Abilities connect in this way, each individual's abilities are magnified. Synergy is created, and the result is considerably better than either person could have achieved alone.

When people begin to discover and focus on their Unique Abilities, they suddenly find themselves drawing a host of dynamic and capable new people into their lives, and seeing new things in the people they already know. Watch what happens to you after you do the exercises in Chapter 2 and begin to articulate your Unique Ability. See what opportunities and connections arise in what might seem to be unlikely places and situations.

Unique does not mean isolated or alone.

The Unique Ability of others.

It's a paradox that in order to spend more time in your Unique Ability, you have to work with other people to achieve the greatest result. Unique does not mean isolated or alone. Quite the opposite. Now that you've begun to see and understand your own Unique Ability, you'll find yourself better able to recognize and appreciate others' Unique Abilities as well. This will give you access to the vast and still largely untapped resource of other people's talents and passions. The amount of energy that's available when you pull together several Unique Abilities around a big, inspiring vision is often astonishing. Magic can be created when people with complementary talents contribute their passions, capabilities, and creativity to create a shared result. Each member of the team can take their portion of the project far beyond expectations, which, in turn, inspires even greater creativity from the rest. It may be a cliché, but this is how "dream teams" are formed. Unique Ability teamwork creates an "upward spiral" of energy, enthusiasm, respect, and creativity. Following are some tips on how to create a successful Unique Ability Team.

Magic can be created when people with complementary talents contribute their passions, capabilities, and creativity to create a shared result.

The Unique Ability Team™.

To be able to effectively spend larger amounts of time in your Unique Ability and use it to create bigger results, you must partner with others. Ideally, surround yourself with a team of people who are talented at and passionate about all the things that need to be done that are not your Unique Ability. We call this a Unique Ability Team. The Unique Ability Team provides a system of support to free you up from all those activities and tasks that drain you of energy, and for which you have limited creativity.

Harnessing passion.

A Unique Ability Team is a heady environment to be in. When everyone is able to commit the full force of their talents and emotions to an endeavor, there's tremendous excitement and possibility. More important, however, the results are exponential. Because, by definition, Unique Ability activities are those things which we do very well with ease, big results become possible because no one is going against their grain. No one is fighting a part of themselves to be successful. Everyone is contributing what they love to do and are best at towards a common goal. It's a very efficient way to operate. There's very little managing of people's behavior to make sure they've done what they were supposed to do. You only need to provide direction so people know how to apply their energies and talents.

Creating the team.

The key requirements for creating a Unique Ability Team are clear results, clear communication, a clear process, and an awareness of Unique Ability.

- ## Clear results.

  For everyone on the team to be working together successfully, they have to know what they are working towards. Having a compelling goal and vision will engage the right people's excitement and enthusiasm. If you're trying to attract people to work with you, figure out what result you're trying to achieve and articulate it clearly, with passion. What are you building? What are you creating? Why are you doing what you're doing?

  At The Strategic Coach, we use a tool called The R-Factor Question™ to elicit this information. It goes like this: "If we were meeting here three years from today, looking back to today, what has to have happened for you to feel happy with your progress?" There are three important elements to this relationship question: It's set in the future, it's only about you and how you feel, and it's based on progress. By setting it in the future, you have to put yourself there, imagine what's happened, and only then figure out what you did to get there. Second, you're the expert on your future — not someone else. Too often, we buy into other people's pictures of our future, not our own. Third, it's about progress, not perfection. How you envision making progress is the essence of this question. Again, you're the only person with the answers. It's a powerful question to answer, and a powerful question to ask.

When you're looking for people to partner with, share your answer to this question. The people who get excited about your vision are the ones who will likely be good team members. Keep in mind that sharing your vision works for your goals at work, in your community, for group projects at school, with your church, and with your family.

You can also ask The R-Factor Question of people you're considering adding to your team. See if they have an answer and, if so, if it aligns with yours. Many people won't, and you'll need to give them some help and time to answer.

To keep people excited
and aligned, regular, effective
communication is key.

- **Clear communication.**
  Communication with other team members, no matter the type of team, is both challenging and important. To be able to contribute their Unique Abilities and support yours, all team members need to be clear on the vision and up-to-date on the progress and changes that inevitably happen in any project or process. You'll find that you can achieve much

better results as a team if all members are clear on how best to communicate with each other. Knowing how people prefer to give and receive communication (e.g. in person, via e-mail, or voicemail), how much information they like when being asked to do something, and how they like to be informed when a task is complete, will help avoid misunderstandings and reduce stress for all. You'll also have to consider how to keep team members informed about the big picture as it evolves. Assuming that certain people don't need to know everything is a sure way to disengage their passion from the bigger vision that may have attracted them in the first place. To keep people excited and aligned, regular, effective communication is key.

- **Clear process.**
  One of the things that's most important when you're putting together your team is to figure out who's going to do what, and when. A simple way to do this is to list all of the activities needed to achieve a particular result, and then to identify the best person to do each task. You want someone who minimally has an excellent ability, if not a Unique Ability. Anything less will likely create a bottleneck.

- **Unique Ability awareness.**
  In Chapter 2, we went over how to discover and describe your Unique Ability. What's required for a Unique Ability Team is that everyone knows, or is in the process of discovering, their Unique Ability. A lack of self-awareness will prevent people from actually doing what they're best at, and from making the best contribution. It's important to realize here just how powerfully

---

When you do something exceptionally well and obviously enjoy it, you radiate a kind of energy that people are naturally drawn to.

people's attachment to status can interfere with contributing their Unique Ability. For example, at a marketing communications company of one of our clients, everyone wanted to be an Account Manager. In advertising, that's where the status is, the glamour, and, presumably, the monetary rewards as well. However, very few actually had the right set of talents and strengths for that role. There were some other roles that desperately needed filling, like that of organizing and structuring work systems, but no one would volunteer because it didn't fit their picture of success. When we met to work with them to discuss Unique Ability, none of them seemed particularly interested. Not surprisingly, about six months later, most of the team had been replaced by people more committed to creating value using talents and strengths than to achieving status.

A Unique Ability community.

The teams you work with, formally or informally, are only a small part of the broader community in which you live your life. Your Unique Ability has the potential to have an impact on a much larger number of people, and many other people's Unique Abilities will have an impact on you. As you get focused on developing the talents that you're passionate about, it's common to find that you're most interested in being around other talented people who are also passionate about what they do. This becomes the basis for a new kind of community — one centered around a commitment to Unique Ability. You may ask, "How do I find people like this?" The answer lies partially in letting your own Unique Ability show. Unique Ability in action is very attractive. When you do something exceptionally well and obviously enjoy it, you radiate a kind of energy that people are naturally drawn to. It takes them back to times when they've felt the same way, or makes them wish they knew your secret. Don't keep it a secret. If you want to grow your Unique Ability community, let others know what you're passionate about and find out what they love to do and where their talents lie. Share the concept of Unique

Ability with them and you'll receive the benefits of getting to know more about them and growing the pool of Unique Abilities you have to draw on to create results and to refer to others.

The more, the better.

One of the strengths of a Unique Ability community is the number and diversity of Unique Abilities available. The more, the better. The more people's Unique Abilities you recognize, the more resources you'll have at your fingertips in any situation and the more unique experiences you can create. Isn't it great, when you have a problem, to know that you can contact someone who would love to provide a fantastic solution for you? Likewise, others in your Unique Ability community can ensure that you get a variety of interesting and rewarding opportunities to use your Unique Ability. But they can only do this if they know what it is. Having a Unique Ability philosophy gives you the freedom to draw on others' talents without feeling guilty or self-serving. People want to be "used," and you're providing a way for them to express their talents and passion.

What if the world operated this way?

Think for a moment what it would be like if the whole world operated this way. If everyone could access everyone else's Unique Abilities when they needed them, people would be much happier, more energized, and better served. Creativity would blossom in areas we can't even imagine, as people's Unique Abilities in an infinite number of areas are given the opportunity to develop in new and exciting ways. Many of the negative by-products that result from people feeling bored, trapped, unappreciated, unfulfilled, or misunderstood would diminish. The realization of this vision begins with individuals creating and growing Unique Ability communities that will naturally link to form a growing informal network of like-minded people. There are already people all over the world who are aware of Unique Ability and who are sharing it because of the benefits it brings to themselves and to others. You are now part of that community.

A different world view.

Throughout history, people have been using their Unique Abilities, without being completely conscious of them, to create outstanding results with seemingly little effort. People's Unique Abilities have enabled them to achieve extraordinary progress in technology, knowledge, art, social sciences, personal relationships, and virtually every area of human endeavor because they had superior skill, driven by a unique passion to advance further than anyone had ever thought possible in a particular area. Every day, people's Unique Abilities shine in a myriad of situations, giving others reasons to praise them, be grateful to them, reward them, and to want to pursue stronger relationships with them. At the same time, every day, people struggle to find the energy to do things that are not their Unique Abilities, that drain their energy, and lower their confidence, that leave them looking to escape to a place where life offers greater enjoyment, excitement, possibility, satisfaction, and rewards. Consciousness of Unique Ability allows people to purposefully create the life they want.

Freedom and happiness.

Unique Ability is also irrepressible. If you look at the history of regimes that had to resort to increasing degrees of force and restriction of freedoms to stay in power, you will see that a common feature is that they were built on the suppression of Unique Ability. Structures that do not support and draw from the strength of people's unique passions and capabilities tend to become increasingly difficult to maintain, requiring greater and greater restrictions on individual freedoms. On the other hand, structures that reward and support the development of Unique Ability tend to increase the freedom of participants in ways that may even expand people's notion of freedom and what's possible. The more an individual's life is focused around their Unique Ability in these structures, the more freedom they have. Freedom allows for greater self-expression, which, in turn, leads to the possibility of true lasting happiness.

When we interviewed people for this book, the same sentiment came up over and over again: "Finding and focusing on my Unique Ability was tremendously, exhilaratingly liberating. It gave me the clarity and the permission to stop doing things that were not giving me energy and allowed me to focus on what I'm really best at and love to do." The results spoke for themselves in every case, and none of our interviewees would ever consider going back to the way their lives were before.

We all have the choice.

Though it's not what most of us learn growing up, we each have the capacity and the opportunity to create a supportive environment for the development of our Unique Ability. Every one of us also has the opportunity to develop a life in which the world rewards us for pursuing our natural talents and passions, and through doing so, to make a contribution that has never been seen before. The more we recognize Unique Ability as a basic human characteristic and a tremendous resource available to be tapped, the easier it is to create these environments and reap their infinite benefits.

> *If one advances confidently in the direction of his dreams and endeavors to live the life which he has imagined, he will meet with success in common hours.*
>
> **Henry David Thoreau**

Write to us.

Let us know about the difference Unique Ability makes in your life.

Unique Ability

c/o The Strategic Coach

33 Fraser Street, Suite 201

Toronto, Ontario

Canada

M6K 3J9

Or e-mail us at *uniqueability@strategiccoach.com*

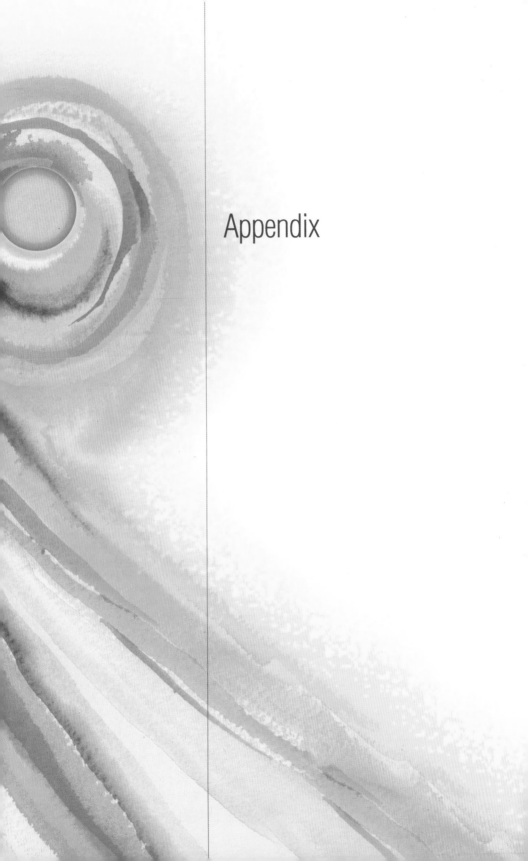

Appendix

Unique Ability

Creating The Life You Want

Appendix

*R*ecommended **Resources.**

The Kolbe Index.

The Kolbe A Index measures your instinctive method of operation, one that allows you to be most productive and satisfied. To complete a Kolbe profile, go to *www.kolbe.com* and click on the Kolbe A Index. Answer the 36 questions, "If free to be myself, I would ...." Respond according to how you would naturally act. Don't over-analyze. Don't let anyone else influence your answers or interpret the questions for you. The results will give you a startlingly accurate picture of what you will and won't do — your striving instincts. When you operate according to your natural instincts, you achieve your best results easily and quickly.

> *Success is the freedom to be yourself.*
>
> **Kathy Kolbe**

StrengthsFinder.

To complete the StrengthsFinder profile, obtain your unique identification number by purchasing the book *Now, Discover Your Strengths.* This number allows you access to the StrengthsFinder profile on the Internet. You can then read about your top five themes and learn how to leverage them for powerful results.

Now, Discover Your Strengths by Marcus Buckingham and Donald O. Clifton. Published by The Free Press. 2001.

On the process of discovering her Unique Ability: "It was difficult at first, because I was so blind to what I really do well. But with Kolbe and StrengthsFinder — those two things really helped. And then just sending out the letters and getting the feedback from colleagues, from people I worked with a long time ago and to this day, and then friends and family — that was very helpful. They couldn't really define my Unique Ability, … It took me six to eight months to say, 'Okay, that's what it is.'"

Colleen Bradley

Anatomy of a Unique Ability — Kara W.

The following example is a more in-depth explanation of one person's Unique Ability. Based on the answers Kara received when she asked The Unique Ability Question, along with her Kolbe profile, her StrengthsFinder, and her own personal experience, Kara came up with the following set of best habits and Unique Ability Statement. This example is intended to help you gain insight on how to integrate the results from various tools into The Unique Ability Discovery Process.

Kolbe A Index: 6644 Mediator profile
StrengthsFinder: Learner, Futuristic, Activator, Achiever, Strategic

Kara's 10 Best Habits:
1. I always assess the situation and figure out my best fit.
As a mediator, Kara can respond to her environment based on what's needed. She can respond on a physical level or an emotional one, whatever the situation requires. If you ask her friends to describe her, they'd each give you a different answer. For some, she is the "funny one," for others, the "stable one." Depending on the roles that are already being played by the people involved, she will adapt to fill the void. The worst thing for her is to not feel useful. Whenever she feels this way, she excuses herself from the situation.

2. I always strive for balance.

Kara easily and naturally sees when people or situations are "out of balance" and could end up in conflict. She surrounds herself with people who will give her a sense of balance, or she will create it herself. This is really important for her to be able to create her best results.

3. I always analyze my physical environment.

When Kara enters an environment, she always notices the details of a space; the environment has an impact on her emotionally. Aesthetics are extremely important to Kara. She can feel inspired by what she considers "beauty." She also enjoys learning about a person from the environment they've created because she is able to glean important clues from the details. Her goal is to create a safe and warm environment, and she considers that people will get to know her by the space she has created.

4. I always am true to myself.

This is based on a value learned from her dad, and later from her husband. She always tries to get to the truth of each situation to see if it fits with her core values. She needs to understand it and see if it works for her. She does an internal check, then looks to see if she needs to adjust her actions or her decisions.

5. I always laugh at things to enjoy life.

Kara's mom always said, "You may as well laugh, otherwise you'll cry." It's her philosophy for living life and her way of coping with challenges. She believes that it's a real test of character if people can laugh at their own foibles. It's just part of being human. She tries to step back and look at the big picture so she can stop the seriousness and perceive experiences in a lighter way.

6. I always organize myself.

Kara creates systems to keep herself organized, and needs to do so to be productive. She can't necessarily create systems for others, but she can accommodate systems that are already created.

7. I always learn by trying.

Kara has a love of learning. She has an attitude that you may as well try things out in order to learn from them. She has a need to challenge herself for personal, intellectual, and physical growth. Ambition is also tied in here, and learning is key to her success. She always needs to have something on her plate to strive for, a goal to accomplish.

8. I always see the end result and think it through to a plausible solution.

When faced with a request or a problem to solve, Kara experiences a "flash" in her head of the end result. She will assess the situation, and if she's excited and engaged, she will get a very clear picture of what it looks like and how to get there. If it's at all possible, it will happen. This is her form of problem solving.

9. I always choose my commitments carefully and then follow through.

Because Kara's sense of self is reflected in her achievements, she is careful to think things through thoroughly before she commits. It's very important for her to keep her word and to be able to create a high-quality result, so she chooses her commitments wisely. The results produced are a direct representation of who she is.

10. I always insist on quality.

Kara believes that if you're going to produce something, it's really important that it's as high quality as possible. She expects a lot of others and herself. When she's passionate, she will do anything to create a great result.

These 10 Best Habits are a crucial part of Kara's success and ability to create her best results. She needs to work and live in an environment that supports her way of being and allows her to live by her values and best actions.

Kara's Unique Ability Statement:
After creating her 10 Best Habits, Kara continued the Unique Ability process and, over time, created the following statement to summarize her Unique Ability:

> ***My Unique Ability is responding to people by visualizing their future and strategizing a plan to achieve a creative solution.***

This statement takes the key words from her 10 Best Habits and combines them to describe the essence of Kara's talent combined with her passion. Each word means something special to Kara and has been chosen specifically to best reflect who she is. Here's the breakdown of her statement:

Unique Ability = Talent + Passion

Kara's Talent:
- "responding to people" — Kara's Mediator Kolbe profile describes her way of operating. She can respond with facts, systems or plans, ideas and innovations, or in tangible ways. Kara uses her energy in whatever way is required in the situation. This is a great asset to a team, as she fills in where needed, and translates between people who operate very differently, because she understands both sides. She responds to people's requests, to different situations, and to the environment around her.

- "visualizing their future" — If you read the description of "Futuristic" in *Now, Discover Your Strengths*, you will see that this strength involves asking, "Wouldn't it be great if . . ." to come up with a future vision. This is part of Kara's talent in her everyday life.

- "strategizing a plan" — Kara has a talent for thinking through to a plausible solution. She visualizes the end result and then creates a plan to navigate the obstacles.

Kara's Passion:

- "to achieve a creative solution" — Kara's "Achiever" strength from StrengthsFinder indicates her need for accomplishment. She is passionate about getting a result and about making a contribution. Kara is a creative person and expresses herself in many different creative ways.

Knowing this crucial information about Kara is extremely valuable when working with her or being in a relationship with her. Kara operates at her best when allowed to be herself. She communicates her values through her best actions in the hope that others will align with them. When operating in her Unique Ability, Kara can make her greatest contribution.

It feels amazing to know your Unique Ability! I go around every day and try and figure out how I could use these skills to better the world!

Kara W.

About
The Strategic
Coach

Unique Ability

Creating The Life You Want

About The Strategic Coach®

*T*he Strategic Coach Program™.

Dan Sullivan is known throughout the world as an innovator and visionary whose ideas have set the standard for others in the entrepreneurial coaching industry. The Strategic Coach Program, co-founded in 1989 with his wife and partner, Babs Smith, was the first coaching program exclusively for entrepreneurs, and remains the most innovative in terms of its ability to help participants make successive quantum leaps toward increasingly greater personal and professional goals.

Strategic Coach® clients today not only significantly increase their income and time off, they build strong, future-focused companies that leave their competition behind. Many have set new standards in their industries and made significant contributions to their communities through the increased focus, resources, and creativity gained by participating in the Program. Because of these results in all areas of life, most participants continue year after year. They comment that, as their dreams grow, the Program grows with them.

The Strategic Coach Inc.

The Strategic Coach is an organization created by entrepreneurs, for entrepreneurs. The company operates using the same philosophy, tools, and concepts taught in The Strategic Coach Program, and has grown more than ten times in the past eight years. With over 100 entrepreneurially-minded team members and two offices, one in Toronto and one in Chicago, the company continues to grow and enrich its offerings to an expanding, global client base. Currently, over 3,000 successful and highly motivated entrepreneurs from over 60 industries and a dozen countries attend Strategic Coach workshops on a quarterly basis.

If you would like more information on The Strategic Coach, its programs for entrepreneurs at all levels of success, and its many products for entrepreneurial thinkers, please call 416.531.7399 or 1.800.387.3206. Or visit *www.strategiccoach.com*

Notes

Notes